I0836905

THE FIRST BANK OF NEW YORK BUILDING ON PRESENT LOCATION, 48 WALL ST.

*Corner-stone laid June 22, 1797.*

# A HISTORY

OF

# The Bank of New York

1784-1884

Compiled from Official Records
and Other Sources at the
Request of the
Directors

BY

HENRY W. DOMETT

FOURTH EDITION

DEDICATED TO

MR. CHARLES E. BILL

SENIOR DIRECTOR

# Preface

A CENTURY has passed since the organization of the Bank of New York, and the board of directors have deemed it proper that some account of the origin and progress of the institution should be published in a suitable form for preservation. As the bank is the oldest institution of the kind in the State, and one of the oldest in the country, its existence covers a period of great changes in the financial policy and condition of the United States, and of severe trials in the business world. No attempt has been made to treat of these, except so far as the Bank of New York has been affected by them.

A greater degree of interest naturally attaches to the early history of the bank than to the events of a later day, with which the reader is more familiar, and a larger proportion of space is therefore given to it in the narrative.

In the appendix will be found some documents which are referred to in the earlier part of the history, and others which will interest those who have been in any way connected with the institution. Among these is a list of the presidents, cashiers, and directors of the bank from its foundation to the present time.

# Preface

The fac-similes of some of the notes issued by the bank at different periods of its existence, and of the checks drawn upon it by Talleyrand and Aaron Burr, will also, it is believed, be found of interest to the reader.

The compiler of this volume desires to acknowledge the valuable aid he has received from Mr. Richard B. Ferris, the vice-president of the bank, who has furnished a large proportion of the statistics, and to whose diligent and intelligent research much of the interest of the narrative is due. Acknowledgments are also due to Mr. John Austin Stevens, from whose published volumes the material for the account of the condition of the city at the time of the organization of the bank, and also for the sketches of the early officers of the institution, was gathered; to General James Watts De Peyster, through whose kind offices a portrait of General Alexander McDougall, the first president of the bank, was obtained, and also to the Honorable William G. Thompson, of Detroit, for the use of the portrait; to Mr. C. V. Quilliard for the use of a miniature of Gulian Verplanck; to Mr. Matthew Clarkson for the steel engravings of his grandfather, Matthew Clarkson; to Miss Ann Wilkes for the use of a portrait of her father, Charles Wilkes; to Mr. D. Colden Murray for the use of a portrait of Isaac Roosevelt; to Mrs. James Suydam for the use of a portrait of Cornelius Heyer; to Mr. William

Oothout for the use of a portrait of his father, John Oothout; to Mr. J. W. Halsey for photographs of Anthony P. Halsey; and to Messrs. Harper & Brothers for the use of a wood-cut of the Walton House.

H. W. D.

*May*, 1884.

# Contents

# Contents

## CHAPTER III

### 1784–1791



## CHAPTER IV

### 1791–1795

# Contents

CHAPTER V

1796–1811



CHAPTER VI

1812–1824

# Contents

## CHAPTER VII

1825–1851



## CHAPTER VIII

1852–1884

## APPENDIX

# List of Illustrations

# A History of the Bank of New York

## CHAPTER I

### 1780–1784

*Condition of the Country previous to the Organization of the Bank.— The Currency employed.— Banking in the United States prior to 1784.— Organization of the Pennsylvania Bank.— The Bank of North America.— Its Usefulness and Success.— Schemes for a Land Bank in New York.— Alexander Hamilton's Opposition to the Project.— Proposals for a Bank with Specie Capital.— Meeting of Subscribers to the Bank of New York.— Election of Officers, March 15, 1784.— Hamilton's Connection with the Enterprise.— His Letter in Relation to it.*

THE Bank of New York began its existence under conditions that are interesting from several points of view. The state of the country at that time, as well as of the city that has since grown to such proportions, the reputation of the eminent statesman whose name is associated with the beginning of the enterprise, and the fact that the Bank of New York was the first institution of the kind organized in this State, give to its early history a peculiar importance.

The country had just concluded, in 1783, a long and exhausting struggle with Great Britain; and when peace was declared, its financial condition was far from satisfactory. Great suffering had been caused by the depreciation of the Continental currency, which, having become worthless, had at last ceased to circulate. It was estimated that the depreciation and repudiation of the Continental bills of credit had imposed a tax upon the country amounting to seventy millions of specie dollars. Besides the paper currency authorized by Congress, all the States had issued bills of their own; although in some of them the obligations had been called in and funded at their nominal value. Yet, although the expedients which had been resorted to had proved to be unsuccessful, some of the States continued to make experiments in finance which did not depend upon specie as a basis.

In the State of New York a good deal of gold and silver was in circulation, and for some years the amount had been increasing. This was in consequence of the large payments by the English army at New York, the remittances of gold and silver made by France to the army and navy here, and by considerable importations from Havana and elsewhere.

For several years after the war the currency was expressed in pounds, shillings, and pence. The money of account of the United States, the dollar, dime, cent, and mill, was legally adopted in New York by an act passed by the Legislature, January 27, 1797, which provided that a dollar should be equivalent to "four tenths of a pound," and fractions thereof in proportion. The "Lyon dollar," which was introduced by the Dutch, and which was for some time during the Colonial period the only legal tender, had entirely disappeared. But in its place had come guineas, and doubloons, and pistoles, and Johannes pieces, and moidores, and sequins. The dollar was therefore only a money of account; and, like the *mark banco* of Hamburg, was a fictitious symbol by which all others were measured.

The history of banking in the United States before the establishment of the Bank of New York is a brief one. The Pennsylvania Bank, which was organized in Philadelphia during the Revolutionary War, was founded for the purpose of facilitating the operations of the government in transporting supplies for the army. It began its useful work in 1780, and continued in existence until after the close of the war; finally closing its affairs toward the end of the year 1784.

But the need was felt of a national bank which should not only aid the government on a large scale by its money and credit, but should extend facilities to individuals, and thereby benefit the community as well as the State. Through the influence and exertions of Robert Morris, then Superintendent of Finance for the United States, the Bank of North America, at Philadelphia, was organized with a capital of $400,000. It was incorporated by Congress in December, 1781, and by the State of Pennsylvania a few months afterward. Its success was immediate and complete. It not only rendered valuable and timely aid to the United States Government and to the State of Pennsylvania, but it greatly assisted in restoring confidence and credit to the commercial community, and afforded facilities to private enterprise that were especially welcome. So profitable were the transactions of the bank while it was rendering such services to the country and to individuals, that, during the years 1783 and 1784, it declared annual dividends averaging fourteen per cent. This result was so satisfactory to the stockholders that in February a new subscription of one thousand shares, of $500 a share, was speedily taken up. A scheme for another bank, to be called the Bank of Pennsylvania, was soon set on foot; but by an arrangement which gave to the projectors of the enterprise an interest in the additional capital of the original bank, the rivalry was avoided. The par value of the stock being reduced, the capital of the bank amounted to $830,000.

The success of the Bank of North America, and the advantages which the citizens of Philadelphia enjoyed from the facilities it offered them, naturally suggested the founding of a similar enterprise in the city of New York. On the 12th of February, 1784, an article appeared in the New York "Packet," then a semiweekly paper, setting forth the advantages of a bank, and proposing the establishment of an institution to be called the Bank of the State of New York, with a capital of $750,000, in shares of $1000 each. The management was to be in the hands of a governor and six directors, who were to serve without compensation until the first dividend was declared. Two of the directors and the governor were to be in constant attendance at the bank, and no money was to be paid out without their consent. The subscribers were to pay one third of their subscriptions in cash, and for the other two thirds landed security was to be given by mortgage or deed of trust. No lands out of New York and New Jersey were to be accepted, and all lands were to be appraised at not more than two thirds of their value. The directors could borrow to the extent of one third of the value of the lands in case they found it necessary to increase the cash resources of the bank, but no further.

The folly of this enterprise and the danger to the community which would attend it were soon pointed out to the public by several writers, in the papers of the day. It was shown that a land bank would not answer the purposes of the merchants, that the public would not deposit their money in a bank which circulated more paper than was in due proportion to the specie actually held by the company, and that in time of trouble the bank could afford no assistance to individuals or to the State. It was also maintained that the hope of deriving any interest from landed property by this means would be disappointed. For as it would finally be necessary to base the circulation upon the stock of specie on hand, the landed security would be unavailable. Others took the ground that such an institution would be the beginning of a landed aristocracy in this country.

Alexander Hamilton joined in the opposition to the scheme, and in the following extract from a letter to J. B. Church, dated New York, March 10, 1784, refers particularly to it: —

"In my last to you I informed you that a project for a land bank had been set on foot by Mr. Sayre, as the ostensible parent; but that I had reason to suspect the Chancellor [Livingston] was the true father. The fact has turned out as I supposed; and the Chancellor, with a number of others, has since petitioned the Legislature for an exclusive charter for the proposed bank. I thought it necessary, not only with a view to your project, but for the sake of the commercial interests of the State, to start an opposition to this scheme; and took occasion to point out its absurdity and inconvenience to some of the most intelligent merchants, who presently saw the matter in a proper light, and began to take measures to defeat the plan.

"The Chancellor had taken so much pains with the country members, that they all began to be persuaded that the land bank was the true philosopher's stone that was to turn all their rocks and trees into gold; and there was great reason to apprehend a majority of the Legislature would have adopted his views. It became necessary to convince the projectors themselves of the impracticability of their scheme; and to counteract the impressions they had made by a direct application to the Legislature."

The agitation of the subject resulted in a project for a bank which should be founded on a more solid basis. The following notice appeared in the New York "Packet" of February 23d:—

BANK

It appearing to be the disposition of the gentlemen in this city to establish a bank on liberal principles, the stock to consist of specie only, they are therefore hereby invited to meet to-morrow evening, at six o'clock, at the Merchants' Coffee-House, where a plan will be submitted to their consideration.

As a result of this call a meeting of the principal merchants and citizens was held at the Coffee-House on the 24th, and another on the 26th, of February. General Alexander McDougall was made chairman, and a series of proposals for the establishment of a bank were read and unanimously agreed to. They provided that the capital stock of the bank should consist of five hundred thousand dollars in gold or silver, divided into one thousand shares of five hundred dollars each; that as soon as five hundred shares should be subscribed for, a general meeting of the subscribers should be held to choose a president, twelve directors, and a cashier, and to invest them with the proper authority; that at all meetings of the subscribers or stockholders, every subscriber or stockholder having one or more shares, to the number of four, should have one vote for each share; a subscriber for six shares should have five votes, one for eight shares six votes, and one for ten shares seven votes; but no stockholder should have more than seven votes, be the number of his shares ever so great. A dividend should be made at the end of twelve months, and every six months afterward; and no subscriber or stockholder should be answerable for the debts of the bank beyond the amount of his stock. The proprietors of the bank, wishing to encourage trade, proposed to establish the rate of discount at six per cent. per annum.

The following gentlemen were unanimously appointed a committee to receive subscriptions: —

| | |
|---|---|
| SAMUEL FRANKLIN, | COMFORT SANDS, |
| HENRY REMSEN, | THOMAS B. STOUGHTON, |
| WILLIAM MAXWELL, | ALDERMAN NEILSON. |

Subscription books were also lodged with John Alsop, Broadway, Robert Bowne, No. 39 Queen Street, and Nicholas Low, No. 27 Water Street.

The opportunity of subscribing to a bank upon so substantial a basis was quickly embraced by the public, and five hundred shares having been taken, a meeting of the stockholders was called to be held at the Coffee-House at ten A. M. on Monday, the 15th of March, 1784, to elect a president, cashier, and twelve directors.

At the meeting held pursuant to this notice, a ballot

was taken, which resulted in the choice of the following officers: —

General ALEXANDER McDOUGALL, *President.*

| | |
|---|---|
| SAMUEL FRANKLIN, | WILLIAM MAXWELL, |
| ROBERT BOWNE, | NICHOLAS LOW, |
| COMFORT SANDS, | DANIEL McCORMICK, |
| ALEXANDER HAMILTON, | ISAAC ROOSEVELT, |
| JOSHUA WADDINGTON, | JOHN VANDERBILT, |
| THOMAS RANDALL, | THOMAS B. STOUGHTON, |

*Directors.*

WILLIAM SETON, *Cashier.*

The enterprise had made some progress before Alexander Hamilton was solicited to become connected with it. It appears that he had already been interested in a similar project which had been set on foot by other persons. In the letter already quoted from, he says, referring to the defeat of the scheme for a land bank: —

"Some of the merchants, to effect these purposes, set on foot a subscription for a money bank, and called upon me to subscribe. I was a little embarrassed how to act, but upon the whole I concluded it best to fall in with them, and endeavor to induce them to put the business upon such a footing as might enable you, with advantage, to combine your interests with theirs; for since the thing had been taken up upon the broad footing of the whole body of the merchants, it appeared to me that it never would be your interest to pursue a distinct project in opposition to theirs; but that you would prefer, so far as you might choose to employ money in this way, to become purchasers in the general bank. The object, on this supposition, was to have the bank founded on such principles as would give you a proper weight in the direction. Unluckily, for this purpose, I entered rather late into the measure; proposals had been agreed upon, in which, among other things, it was settled that no stockholder, to whatever amount, should have more than seven votes, which was the number to which a holder of ten shares was to be entitled. At an after-meeting of some of the most influential characters, I engaged them so far to depart from this ground as to allow a vote for every five shares above ten.

"The stockholders have since thought proper to appoint me one of their directors. I shall hold it until Wadsworth and you come out, and, if you choose to become parties to this bank, I shall make a vacancy for one of you. I enclose you the constitution, and the names of the president, directors, and cashier.

"An application for a charter has been made to the Legislature, with a petition against granting an exclusive one to the land bank. The measures which have been taken appear to have had the effect upon the minds of the partisans of the land bank."

A Hamilton

# CHAPTER II

## 1784

*Constitution of the Bank of New York. — The Officers of the Institution. — General Alexander McDougall. — William Seton. — Mr. Seton's Visit to Philadelphia. — Payment of Subscription to the Bank. — Opposition to the Enterprise. — Objections urged against it. — Commencement of Business at the Bank. — Rules and Regulations adopted for its Customers. — Rates fixed for Gold and Silver Coin. — Paper Currency of Pennsylvania and New Jersey in Circulation.*

THE constitution which was adopted at the meeting of subscribers embodied the conditions set forth in the original call, but with some important modifications. The document was written by Alexander Hamilton, and, as given in his complete works, edited by his son, John C. Hamilton, is as follows: —

CONSTITUTION OF THE BANK OF NEW YORK.

ARTICLE 1. — That the Bank shall be called by the name and title of the Bank of New York.

ARTICLE 2. — That the capital stock shall consist of five hundred thousand dollars in gold or silver, divided into one thousand shares of five hundred dollars each share; and that a majority of all directors may, at their discretion, open new subscriptions for increasing the capital stock, where they shall judge it for the interest of the Bank so to do, provided the said new subscriptions do not exceed the sum of five hundred thousand dollars.

ARTICLE 3. — That thirteen directors be annually chosen

by a majority of votes, who are to have the sole conduct and management of the Bank. At the first general election, the president and cashier are to be elected by the subscribers to the Bank, but forever afterward the thirteen directors are to choose a president from among themselves; and the cashier, as well as every other person employed in the Bank, is to be appointed and paid by them, and be under their immediate control.

Article 4. — That the first election be on the 15th day of March, 1784; that the next general election for thirteen directors shall be on the second Monday in May, 1785; and so continued yearly, and every year; but in case of any vacancy in the direction by death, resignation, or otherwise, public notice shall be given within one week after such an event, that the vacancy may be filled; the election to be within fourteen days after such notice.

Article 5. — That every holder of one or more shares, to the number of four, shall have one vote for each share. A subscriber of six shares shall have five votes; eight shares, six votes; and ten shares, seven votes; and one vote for every five shares above ten.

Article 6. — That no stockholder, after the first election, shall be entitled to vote, unless such person has possessed the stock three months previous to the day fixed for an election of directors, or any other general purpose. And if any stockholder (who shall have been a resident in this State at least twelve months immediately preceding such election) should be absent, he shall be entitled to vote by proxy, properly appointed; but in no other case shall any vote be admitted by proxy.

Article 7. — That no person shall be eligible to serve in the office of director unless he be a stockholder.

Article 8. — That the board of directors determine the manner of doing business, and the rules and forms to be pursued, appoint and employ the various clerks and servants which they may find necessary, and dispose of the money and credit of the Bank for the interest and benefit of the proprietors; but they are not to employ the money or credit of the Bank in the drawing or negotiating of any foreign bill, or bills of exchange, or advance a loan to any foreign power whatever.

ARTICLE 9. — That if at any time it shall be the opinion of a majority of the directors that any of their body are guilty of neglect of duty, or any malpractice, whereby the interest of the Bank is or may be affected, such majority of the directors, with or without the consent of the president, may advertise for a general meeting of the stockholders, to lay before them a complaint of such neglect of duty, or breach of trust; and if it appears to the stockholders to be well founded, such director or directors may be removed by a majority of votes.

ARTICLE 10. — That if any of the directors shall convert any of the money or property of the Bank to his own particular use, or be guilty of fraud or embezzlement, he shall forfeit his whole share of stock to the company, and be expelled the direction by a majority of all the directors, and thereby rendered incapable of ever serving again in that office.

ARTICLE 11. — That no president or director shall receive any other emolument for his attendance on the duties of the office than such as shall be fixed and agreed to by a majority of votes at a general election.

ARTICLE 12. — That there shall be a meeting of the directors quarterly, for the purpose of regulating the affairs of the Bank, and not less than seven shall constitute a board who may adjourn from time to time, and the president if necessary may call a meeting of the directors at any intermediate time; at every meeting of the directors all questions are to be decided by a majority of votes.

ARTICLE 13. — That the president or a majority of the directors shall have power to call a general meeting of the stockholders by an advertisement in the public papers, whenever it appears to them there is urgent occasion.

ARTICLE 14. — That the cashier and every principal clerk do give a security for their trust to such an amount as a majority of all the directors shall require.

ARTICLE 15. — That all notes issued by the Bank shall be signed by the president for the time being, or any director who may be fixed upon for that purpose, and countersigned by the cashier, or in his absence by a clerk to be appointed by the directors.

ARTICLE 16. — That no stockholder shall be accountable to any individual or the public for money lodged in the Bank for a greater sum than the amount of his stock.

ARTICLE 17. — That such a dividend of the profits of the Bank as a majority of all the directors shall determine to make, shall be declared at least fourteen days previous to the general election in May, 1785; and that all subsequent dividends shall be made half yearly.

ARTICLE 18. — That all shares shall be transferable, such transfer to be made by the proprietor or proprietors, or his, her, or their lawful attorney, in books kept at the Bank for that purpose, which books shall be always kept open at the usual office hours, except on particular days previous to the declaring a dividend, of which due notice shall be given.

ARTICLE 19. — That the president and directors shall petition the Legislature to incorporate the subscribers or stockholders under the name and title of the President, Directors, and Company of the Bank of New York, and to pass laws for inflicting the most exemplary punishment on those who may commit fraud or embezzlement; and also to punish the counterfeiters of bank notes and checks in the like exemplary manner, with such other clauses in the act as they shall judge necessary and proper for the security of the stockholders and the public.

ARTICLE 20. — That this constitution shall be fairly transcribed upon parchment and remain at the Bank; the president and directors when chosen, and prior to the opening of the Bank, shall severally sign and seal the same, and take an oath or affirmation before a magistrate that he will, to the best of his knowledge and abilities, conduct the business of the Bank for the interest and benefit of its proprietors, and agreeable to the true intent and meaning of this constitution, which oath or affirmation shall also be taken by every future director when chosen, and before he enters upon the execution of his trust.

As the newly elected officers of the bank were not familiar with the methods of banking business, Mr. Seton, the cashier, was empowered to go to Philadelphia, with a letter of introduction from Hamilton, and procure the desired information from the Bank of North America.[1]

The new institution was fortunate in the choice of its principal officers, not only on account of their capacity and their fitness for the offices they were to fill, but because they represented two distinct elements in the community at that time.

General Alexander McDougall was born in the island of Islay, Scotland, in 1731, and came with his father to New York when a boy. In his younger days he followed the seas and became master of a small coasting sloop. In 1758 he commanded a privateer called the Tiger; but relinquishing a seafaring life he settled in New York. He was successful in business,

[1] See Appendix.

took an active part in politics, and like many others of foreign birth, warmly espoused the interests of his adopted country. In 1765, at the age of thirty-four, he was one of the most prominent of the "Sons of Liberty." In 1775, when affairs were rapidly approaching a crisis, McDougall was placed at the head of the first of the four patriot regiments raised in New York. On the 9th of August, 1776, he received his commission as brigadier-general, and superintended the embarkation of the Americans in their retreat after the battle of Long Island. He also succeeded General Putnam in command of the Highlands, and was in charge of West Point after Arnold's treachery. He was commissioned as major-general in 1777, and after peace was declared he was elected to the new State Senate. When the Society of the Cincinnati was formed he was chosen as its president. He was a man of strong will, vigorous and fearless in the expression of his opinions on political subjects, and he naturally exerted a considerable influence in the community in which he lived.

William Seton was also a Scotchman by birth, having been born in Fifeshire, Scotland, in 1746. He came to America at an early age, and in 1767 married a daughter of Mr. Richard Curson of Maryland. In 1768 the young merchant was admitted to membership in the Chamber of Commerce, being engaged in the shipping and importing business at Cruger's Dock with his brother-in-law, and at a later period was of the firm

Alex: McDougall

PRESIDENT 1784-1785

of Seton, Maitland & Co. He seems not to have taken an active part in the events which immediately preceded the Revolution. Though moderate in his opinions, his sympathies were evidently with the royal side, and he remained in the city when the British troops took possession in the fall of 1776. His business was probably not prosperous during the war, for in 1777 he was appointed assistant warehouse keeper, an office which he retained until 1780. In 1783, when the new line of French packets began to run to the port of L'Orient, he was placed in charge as deputy agent under the French consul.

He was especially fitted for the office of cashier of the bank by his sterling business qualifications, his diligent, precise, and methodical habits, and by an amiability and courtesy which made him very popular. His appointment as an officer of the bank, with General McDougall, the early leader of the "Sons of Liberty," and a distinguished officer of the Revolution, shows the esteem in which Mr. Seton was held by the liberal party at the close of the war.

On reaching Philadelphia, Mr. Seton found everything at the Bank of North America in a state of great confusion. The opposition to the bank by the projectors of a new institution had resulted in so far reducing the stock of specie as to make it necessary to stop discounting. But an arrangement was made by which those interested in the new bank were allowed to take stock in the Bank of North America, and the serious results which had been anticipated were happily avoided.[1]

The subscription books to the Bank of New York were advertised to be kept open for further subscriptions at the offices of Robert Bowne, Esq., No. 39 Queen Street; Nicholas Low, Esq., 27 Water Street; and Wm. Maxwell, Esq., No. 4 Wall Street.

On the 1st of May, 1784, public notice was given to the subscribers to pay the first moiety of their subscriptions, on the 1st of June, to William Seton, cashier, at No. 67 St. George's Square; and, on the 22d of May, "the president and directors qualified before His Worship, the Mayor, as required by the constitution."

The organization of the bank seems not to have satisfied all the subscribers, for, in Mrs. Elizabeth Holt's New York "Journal and State Gazette," a few days later, one of them complained that the directors did not call a meeting to decide whether or not they would proceed without first obtaining a charter. He says:—

> "I am a subscriber to that institution, and heartily wish that a bank which may have the confidence of the Government, as well as of the merchants of the city, may be established; but unless it can obtain a charter, I cannot consider myself under any obligation to pay in my subscription. When the regulations were published and agreed upon, it was stipulated that no subscriber should be liable for more than his stock. This

[1] See Appendix.

presupposes the grant of a charter; for, without it, this article could not take effect; should the subscription money be at present paid in, the stockholders become to all intents and purposes bankers, and every man is liable — however small his share may be — for all the engagements of the bank to the extent of his whole fortune."

But so desirous was the mercantile community to obtain the facilities of a bank, and so encouraging a prospect of ample returns, in view of the dividends of the bank in Philadelphia, was offered by the enterprise to investors, that it was thought inexpedient to wait for any legislation in the matter. Accordingly, on the 7th of June, the subscriptions having been paid in, and some deposits already having been made, notice was given that the bank would formally commence business on Wednesday, the 9th of June, 1784; and that applications for discount would be received on the succeeding Wednesday. The following rules, to be observed at the bank, were also published:—

"The bank will be open every day in the year, except Sundays, Christmas Day, New Year's Day, Good Friday, the Fourth of July, and general holidays appointed by legal authority.

"The hours of business will be from ten to one o'clock in the forenoon, and from three to five o'clock in the afternoon.

"Discounts will be done on Thursday in every week, and bills and notes brought for discount must be left at the bank on Wednesday morning, under a sealed cover, directed to William Seton, Cashier. The rate of discount is at present fixed at six per cent. per annum; but no discount will be made for longer than thirty days, nor will any note or bill be discounted to pay a former one. Payment must be made in bank notes or specie. Three days of grace being allowed upon all bills, the discount will be taken for the same.

"Money lodged at the bank may be re-drawn at pleasure, free of expense; but no draft will be paid beyond the balance of the account.

"Bills or notes left with the bank will be presented for acceptance, and the money collected free of expense; in case of non-payment and protest, the charge of protest must be borne by the party lodging the bill.

"Payments made at the bank must be examined at the time, as no deficiency suggested afterward will be admitted.

"Gold coin is received and paid at the Bank of New York at the following rates:—

| | | | | | |
|---|---|---|---|---|---|
| A Johannes, | weighing | 18 dwt | | . . . | $16.00 |
| A half " | " | 9 " | | . . . | 8.00 |
| A Spanish doubloon, | " | 17 " | | . . . | 15.00 |
| A double Spanish Pistole, | " | 8 " | 12 gr. | . | 7.48 |
| A Spanish Pistole, | " | 4 " | 6 " | . | 3.72 |
| A British Guinea, | " | 5 " | 6 " | . | 4.64 |
| A British half Guinea, | " | 2 " | 15 " | . | 2.32 |
| A French Guinea, | " | 5 " | 4 " | . | 4.52 |
| A Moidore, | " | 6 " | 18 " | . | 6.00 |
| A Caroline, | " | 6 " | 8 " | . | 4.72 |
| A Chequin, | " | 2 " | 4 " | . | 1.78 |

"An allowance is made on all gold exceeding the above standard at the rate of three pence per grain; on all gold short of the above weight four pence per grain is deducted.

"By order of the Board of Directors,

"ALEXANDER McDOUGALL, *Pres't.*"

Both the Johannes and the moidore were gold coins of Portugal; the Johannes being so called from the figure of King John which it bore. The Caroline was a German coin, and the pistole was of the same value as the Louis d'or. The chequin, sometimes written zeechin, zechin, and sequin, was a gold coin, and had its name from La Zecha, a place in the city of Venice, where the mint was situated. The clipping and sweating of the gold coins in circulation had long been carried on in New York, and as far back as 1770 the Chamber of Commerce had stigmatized it as "an evil and scandalous practice," and had passed a resolution agreeing not to take the light coins, except at a discount of fourpence for each deficient grain. A good deal of trouble was experienced at the bank after it commenced business, from this source, and Hamilton was for some time occupied in devising a method of receiving and paying out gold. This had been done elsewhere by weighing in quantities; a practice which was attended with many difficulties, and for which, in the absence of a national coinage, it was not easy to find a substitute.

The paper currency of Pennsylvania and of New Jersey, which circulated in large quantities in New York, gave a great deal of trouble to the merchants, and the subject was frequently discussed by the Chamber of Commerce. As late as the 3d of April, 1787, a committee was appointed by that body, to consider what countenance should be given to the circulation of the currency of other states, and a report was made that "the Chamber should not for the present interfere in the matter."

## CHAPTER III

### 1784–1791

*Appearance and Condition of the City of New York in 1784. — The First Location of the Bank. — The Walton House. — Annual Meeting of the Stockholders in 1785. — Election of Jeremiah Wadsworth as President. — Death of General Alexander McDougall in 1786. — First Dividend of the Bank. — Annual Meeting in 1786. — Isaac Roosevelt elected President. — Opposition to the Bank. — Success of the Institution. — Emission of Paper Money by the State in 1786. — Action of the Bank respecting it. — Repeated Efforts to obtain a Charter for the Bank. — Petition to the Legislature in 1789 for an Act of Incorporation. — A Charter granted in 1791.*

IT will not be inappropriate to recall the appearance of the city and the condition of affairs at the time when the Bank of New York first opened its doors to the public. The limits of the settled part of the city did not extend beyond Murray Street. According to Mr. John Austin Stevens, the greater part of the population dwelt within a line drawn from the North River at the foot of Reade Street, across the island in an easterly direction to the East River at the foot of Catherine Street. Beyond, on a part of what was called the Out-Ward, was an irregular parallelogram, with Division Street as a base, extending easterly as far as Norfolk Street, and northerly to Hester Street, through which ran the old Bowery Lane to Kingsbridge. The total surface averaged about three quarters of a mile in width, and was embraced within a circumference of about four miles.

The streets throughout the city were irregular, the better class of houses of brick, mostly painted, and with tiled roofs. Water and Queen (now Pearl) streets were low and narrow, poorly paved, with indifferent sidewalks, in some parts with none. They were the chief business streets. Broad Street, which extended from the Exchange, at the water side, to the City Hall, on the corner of Wall Street, was the main avenue. Wall Street was one of the widest streets; the buildings in it were large and elegant. The upper part was occupied by fashionable residences; the lower was exclusively given up to stores and offices, here and there interspersed with lodging-houses. At the corner of Wall and Broad streets stood the City Hall. It was built upon broad open arches through which the pathway lay from street to street. Nearly opposite was the modest dwelling of Alexander Hamilton, upon part of the present site of the Mechanics' Bank. A statue of William Pitt stood at the corner of William Street, mutilated and defaced after his speech against American Independence. Great Dock Street, or that part of Pearl Street between Whitehall and Coenties Slip, had long been the court end of the town, but Wall Street had grown to be a rival as a seat of fashion. Here dwelt the Verplancks, the Ludlows, the Marstons, the Winthrops, the Buchanans, and other well-known families. William Street was the principal street for the retailing of dry goods.

Broadway was then, as now, the backbone or ridge of the island. It was fast growing in favor as the most agreeable part of the city, and the buildings upon it extended from the Bowling Green as far as St. Paul's Church. From the rear of the houses on Broadway gardens were laid out on the slope which ended on a sandy beach, and the street commanded a delightful prospect of the town and the Hudson. Cortlandt Street was the principal street cut through the green embankment, and at its foot were the Bear (now Washington) Market, and the ferry to Powles Hook, now Jersey City.

On the corner of Vesey Street a signboard bore the inscription "Road to Albany," and on the opposite corner, on the house where the "New York Herald" building now stands, a similar sign pointed out to the traveler the "Road to Boston."

At the foot of Maiden Lane stood the Fly Market, so called from "Vly" or valley, its site having originally been a salt meadow. At this point was the ferry to Brooklyn, then a pleasant agricultural town of three or four hamlets or neighborhoods and with some four thousand inhabitants.

It is difficult to estimate accurately the population of New York in 1784. A considerable change had taken place within a year by the emigration of the loyalists, the return of the patriots who had left the city during the war, and the influx of newcomers who were to make the city their home. Two years later, in 1786, the dwelling-houses numbered 3340 according to Noah Webster, a trustworthy authority, and the population 23,604. New York was therefore, at that time, the second city in size in the country; Philadelphia the first, having 40,000 inhabitants; Boston 16,000, Baltimore 15,000, and Charleston 10,000.

The first directory of the city of New York was published in 1786; and a comparison of the little volume with those of the present day strikingly illustrates the growth of the city during the century. In the directory for 1786, which is printed in large type, 33 small pages, 3 x 6 inches, contain the names of 933 residents. The city directory for 1884 contains about 300,029 names, occupying 1940 pages of fine type. Two additional leaves in the directory for 1786 have a list of the inhabitants of Brooklyn numbering 128 names. The Brooklyn directory for 1884 contains 161,238 names in its 1456 pages.

Inland communication for some time after the war was slow and infrequent. In 1787 the Boston stage set out from Hall's Tavern, No. 49 Cortlandt Street, every Monday and Thursday morning, and reached Boston in six days. The fare was four cents per mile. In 1785 the first stages began their trips between New York and Albany. In 1787 two stages set out for

Philadelphia at four o'clock every afternoon, stopping for the night in Newark, and reaching Philadelphia the next day.

A line of packet ships, five in number, was established by French capital in the fall of 1783, and trips were made monthly to the port of L'Orient. The line was under the direction of the Consul-General of France at New York, and the immediate supervision of William Seton, afterward cashier of the Bank of New York. The Black Ball line of packets to England was not established until 1816.

These facts give some idea of the appearance and condition of the city when the first bank was established in it. The original location of the Bank of New York was No. 67 St. George's Square (afterward changed to Franklin Square in honor of Benjamin Franklin), and also known as No. 156 Queen Street, afterward Pearl Street. The building was the well-known Walton House; an edifice of historic interest, and until within a few years one of the relics of old New York. It was a handsome building of yellow Holland brick, with brown-stone lintels and massive walls, fifty feet wide and three stories high, and was entered by a "stoop" raised a few steps above the street. It was built by William Walton in 1752 for a private residence; and few of those who saw the shabby old lodging-house that stood until 1881 opposite the establishment of Messrs. Harper Brothers

THE WALTON HOUSE, IN WHICH THE BANK OF NEW YORK COMMENCED BUSINESS, JUNE 9, 1784.

imagined that it had been one of the elegant mansions of colonial times.

The bank continued to occupy a part of this building until 1787, when it removed to No. 11 Hanover Square, where the Cotton Exchange now stands. This property was bought for five thousand pounds, New York currency. The cashier, Mr. Seton, lived for a time in the building.

At the annual meeting held on the 9th of May, 1785, Jeremiah Wadsworth was elected president, and the following gentlemen, directors:—

| | |
|---|---|
| NICHOLAS LOW, | THOMAS STOUGHTON, |
| JAMES MCCORMICK, | ALEXANDER HAMILTON, |
| SAMUEL FRANKLIN, | ISAAC ROOSEVELT, |
| THOMAS RANDALL, | COMFORT SANDS, |
| ROBERT BOWNE, | JOSHUA WADDINGTON, |
| WILLIAM MAXWELL, | JOHN VANDERBILT. |

Mr. Wadsworth was the friend to whom reference is made in Alexander Hamilton's letter of March 10, 1784. His connection with the bank terminated with the official year.

General McDougall, who declined a reëlection, died on the 9th of June, 1786, and the following tribute to his memory was published in the New York "Packet" of the 12th:—

"In the death of this gentleman, his family lost an affectionate head, his friends a warm and steady friend, and his country a citizen — the dearest object of whose latest moments was the Public Good. A republican by nature and habit, his life has been distinguished by many conspicuous proofs of an ardent and pure attachment to the principles of liberty. . . . He espoused the cause of American liberty in adversity, and was constant to her in all the vicissitudes of her fortune. At the earliest period of the contest he stood foremost, a mark for the indignation of offended power, and in the progress of that contest was ever ready in the field or in the Senate to brave its utmost resentment."

The first dividend made by the bank of which there is any record was one of three per cent. declared on the 25th of April, 1786, payable on the 1st of May; but as it was declared for the six months from the 1st of November, 1785, it is probable that previous dividends had been paid.

In May, 1786, Isaac Roosevelt was elected president, and William Maxwell vice-president. The directors were the same as during the previous year, with the exception of James Buchanan, who was substituted for Jeremiah Wadsworth.

The business of the city as well as of the State had by this time greatly increased. Importations of foreign goods had been large, and the effect was felt throughout the State in the drain of specie which naturally followed. The opponents of the bank took advantage of this state of affairs to charge the institution with having produced it. The direst results to the country were predicted from the establishment of the bank, and the only remedy for the existing evils was maintained to be an emission of paper money by the State. The directors were charged with working in the interest of British capitalists and traders, and with refusing discounts a few days before the sailing of the European packet that they, personally, might profit by the distress thus occasioned. The bank, it was contended, had destroyed private credit as well as that confidence, forbearance, and compassion formerly shown by creditors to their debtors. Such was the result of enforcing the payment of a note at maturity when lodged in the bank. And among the terrible consequences to follow it was predicted that "if their number is not restricted, should banks be permitted in America, after the profits they yield are known, we may not alone have one in every State, but also in every county of the different States."

In spite of the opposition to the bank its business increased. Regular semi-annual dividends of three per cent. were paid until November, 1788, when the dividend was increased to three and a half per cent. for the previous six months. It continued at that rate until the charter was obtained in 1791. But the opponents of the bank succeeded in defeating, until that time, the application to the Legislature for a charter.

A strong pressure had been brought to bear upon the Legislature in favor of an emission by the State of paper money, which should be made a legal tender.

The merchants of New York as a body were opposed

to the scheme, and the Chamber of Commerce had adopted a memorial remonstrating against the passage of any bill to that effect, and setting forth the evil effects of such an issue. But outside of the city there was a belief that financial relief and permanent prosperity would come with an abundance of paper money. The experience of the past had not deterred the people from such a conviction, and several of the States had lately issued bills of credit. Since the adoption of the state constitution of New York only one law of the kind had been passed in the State. This was in 1781, when $411,250 was issued to pay the proportion called for by Congress to pay the expenses of the war. The bill before the Legislature was passed during the session of 1786. It authorized the emission of $200,000 at five per cent. "for the purpose of increasing the currency." This was the last issue of paper money by the State. The Federal Constitution, framed in 1787, contained a clause that "no State shall coin money, emit bills of credit, or make anything but gold or silver coin a tender in payment of debts." The framers of the document thus fixed their condemnation of the old paper-money system, and the people were obliged to look to other agencies for supplying them with a circulating medium more convenient than gold and silver.

In June, 1787, the paper money issued by the State having obtained a considerable circulation, the directors decided to open accounts and make discounts and payments in this currency distinct from those in specie or the bills of the bank. This was continued for several years, and to facilitate the arrangement discounts were done in paper on Tuesdays and in specie on Thursdays.

The efforts which had been made since the organization of the bank to obtain a charter had met with much opposition, and had repeatedly failed. A petition had been presented to the Legislature for a charter at the time of the first meeting of subscribers, but had proved unsuccessful, and another effort was made soon after the bank went into operation. On the 13th of November, 1784, a petition from the president, directors, and stockholders was presented to the Senate, praying for an act of incorporation. Mr. Alexander McDougall was directed to prepare and bring in a bill for that purpose. The bill passed a first and second reading, and was committed to a Committee of the Whole. Action upon it was taken in the Committee of the Whole, and being unfavorably reported to the Senate on the 9th of April, 1785, the bill was rejected.

On the 15th of July, 1789, another petition to the Senate from the president, directors, and stockholders of the bank, asking for its incorporation, was referred to a committee consisting of Messrs. James Duane, Peter Van Ness, and Philip Livingston, who reported favorably, and the petitioners were given leave to bring in a bill. Mr. Duane, in behalf of the petitioners, accordingly brought in a bill, which was read the first time and ordered to a second reading; and a copy of the petition and also of the bill were ordered to be published in one of the public newspapers of New York and Albany previous to the next meeting of the Legislature.

The petition, as printed in the New York "Packet" of October 1, 1789, sets forth the reasons for asking for an act of incorporation:—

*To the Honorable the Legislature of the State of New York:*

The PETITION of the president, directors, and company of the Bank of New York respectfully sheweth: That your petitioners in the year 1784 became subscribers to a bank, which was then instituted in this city, and has been carried on since that period, to the great accommodation of its inhabitants and to the advancement of the commerce of the State at large.

That they flatter themselves (whatever doubts may have been heretofore entertained in regard to the point) their own experience, confirming the experience of other nations, has evinced the utility of institutions of this kind, and has shown that they are worthy the patronage of the government.

That standing on the footing of a private company, in which each member is supposed to be personally responsible for all the engagements entered into, it has been found that many persons who would otherwise be desirous of becoming subscribers are deterred by that circumstance from doing so; whereby the increase of the stock of the bank is obstructed and its operations proportionably confined.

That one essential object of banks is to afford aid to the government in particular exigencies; which object in the present situation of the Bank of New York, from the cause assigned, must either not be answered at all, or not in the degree which is requisite to the due accommodation of the Federal Government.

That while your petitioners are fully persuaded that the Honorable the Legislature will be disposed to promote every proper measure which may conduce to that end, they forbear to do more than to remark that there are obvious reasons which shew that it is peculiarly the interest of the State, at the present juncture, to facilitate the means by which that accommodation may be afforded.

That the incorporation of the Bank of New York is an indispensable step toward enabling it to give any material aid to the government of the United States.

Wherefore, and from the tried utility of the institution in other respects, your petitioners cannot but flatter themselves that the wisdom of the Legislature will discern the expediency of passing an act for that purpose: And they humbly crave leave to present a bill accordingly.

For which, as in duty bound, they will ever pray, etc.

[Signed.]

| | |
|---|---|
| Isaac Roosevelt, | John Murray, |
| Wm. Maxwell, | Samuel Franklin, |
| Daniel McCormick, | Thomas Randall, |
| William Edgar, | Joshua Waddington, |
| Comfort Sands, | Nicholas Low, |
| Robert Bowne, | Thomas Stoughton, |

William Constable.

New York, *3d July, 1789.*

On the 14th of January, 1790, at the second meeting of the thirteenth session of the Senate, the petition of the president, directors, and company of the bank was renewed, and Mr. Livingston, having obtained leave of the Senate, brought in a bill to incorporate the bank.

This bill passed a second reading, and was referred to the Committee of the Whole, in which it was rejected by the casting vote of the chairman. In this rejection the Senate concurred.

The effort to obtain an act of incorporation having thus failed in the Senate, a petition was presented to the Assembly on the 19th of January, 1791. It was referred to a committee, which reported favorably, and the committee was directed to introduce a bill. This passed a second reading, and was committed to the Committee of the Whole. The bill was considered on the 11th and 24th of February and the 1st, 4th, and 7th of March; some amendments were made to it, and it was ordered as amended to be engrossed.

On the 8th of March, 1791, the bill was passed by the Assembly, and Mr. Hoffman and Mr. Pintard were appointed a committee to deliver the bill to the Senate and ask its concurrence. The bill was considered by the Senate on the 9th and 10th of March, and, having been amended, was passed, and Mr. Clinton and Mr. Carpenter were appointed a committee to deliver the bill as amended to the Assembly.

On the 16th of March, 1791, the House of Assembly took up the bill as passed by the Senate, and concurred in all the amendments but one. This action being reported to the Senate, that body receded from its amendment not concurred in by the House. The bill as amended was then passed by both Houses of the Legislature, and became a law on the 21st of March, 1791, by the signature of the governor.[1] This charter was substantially the model upon which all the bank charters granted in the State of New York were framed prior to the year 1825. At that time the form of the acts of incorporation was changed, and more stringent prohibitions and restrictions were enacted by the Legislature.

[1] See Appendix.

# CHAPTER IV

## 1791–1795

*Capital of the Bank. — Its Assets and Liabilities at the Date of Incorporation. — Acceptance of the Charter. — Amount of Bills and Notes discounted. — Election of Gulian Verplanck as President in 1791. — Isaac Roosevelt. — Alexander Hamilton's Relations with the Bank while Secretary of the Treasury. — The Bank of the United States. — A Branch of the Bank in New York in 1792. — Projects for a Rival Bank. — Hamilton's Views respecting it. — Efforts to obtain an Act of Incorporation for it. — Failure of the Scheme. — Deposit in the Bank of New York of Funds belonging to the State in 1792. — Election of a State Director. — Financial Distress in New York in 1791. — Hamilton's Efforts for the Relief of the Merchants. — Loan by the Bank to the Society for Establishing Useful Manufactures. — Resignation of William Seton as Cashier. — Loan by the Bank to the City of Philadelphia in 1793. — Loans to the State of New York and to the United States.*

ON the 1st of May, 1791, the capital of the bank was $318,250. The unpaid moiety of the subscriptions was called in, and on the 1st of July the capital was $495,000. By the 1st of August the balance was paid in, making the capital $900,000.

The following is a statement of the assets and liabilities of the bank at the time it commenced business under the charter, May 1, 1791. It gives some idea of the volume of the bank's business at that time.

SPECIE BANK

| | | | |
|---|---|---|---|
| Bills discounted . . . | $845,940.20 | Capital stock . . . . | $318,250.00 |
| Due from Corporation | 12,222.44 | Notes outstanding . . | 181,254.00 |
| Cash $516,081.87 | | Due depositors . . . | 773,709.67 |
| Less notes | | Profit and Loss . . . | 47,764.84 |
| on hand 53,266.00 | 462,815.87 | | |
| | $1,320,978.51 | | $1,320,978.51 |

PAPER BANK

| | | | |
|---|---|---|---|
| House & lot, Queen St. | £5,248 4 9 | Notes out . . . . | £71,822 0 0 |
| Cash, £115,373 17 11 | | Due depositors . . | 16,920 0 4 |
| Notes | | Profit and loss . . | 6,275 2 4 |
| on hand, 25,605 | 89,768 17 11 | | |
| | £95,017 2 8 | | £95,017 2 8 |

On the 2d of May, 1791, the directors named in the act of incorporation formally accepted the charter, assumed all the existing liabilities of the former company, and reëlected the former officers. Two thousand sheets of circulating notes were ordered to be printed and signed, ready for emission "as quick as possible." The paper on which these notes were printed was made in Philadelphia, and the notes were struck off on a hand-press in the bank.

On the 1st of November, 1791, a dividend of seven per cent. was declared out of the first six months' business of the incorporated bank. During these six months the amount of bills and notes discounted amounted to $10,558,669.59, and the total amount of cash received was $42,681,664.80. These figures illustrate the extent of the mercantile transactions of New York at that period. It will be remembered that no notes or bills were discounted for a longer time than forty-five days, and during the first year of the bank's existence the limit was thirty days.

At the annual election in 1791, Gulian Verplanck was elected president of the bank in place of Isaac Roosevelt, who had declined a reëlection. Mr. Roosevelt's business was that of a sugar refiner, and his store was originally in Wall Street. He was one of the most noted Whigs of the time. He served as one of the General Committee of One Hundred, chosen in May, 1775, to take control of the government. Upon the entry of the British he withdrew from the city. His sacrifices were rewarded by his countrymen, and he was elected to various stations of honor. He represented the city of New York in the convention which met at Kingston in 1777 to form a constitution for this State, and was a member of the New York Convention which assembled at Poughkeepsie in 1786 to deliberate on the adoption of the Constitution of the United States. After peace was declared he served as state senator.

When the Bank of New York occupied the old Walton House, Mr. Roosevelt's sugar refinery was just opposite at No. 159 Queen Street. He had resumed business in partnership with his son. He was president of the New York Hospital from 1790 to 1794, and took a warm interest in its welfare. He died in October, 1797, at the age of sixty-eight years,

Isaac Roosevelt

PRESIDENT 1786-1791

beloved and honored as an excellent citizen and a tried and true patriot.

When the Constitution of the United States went into operation, in 1789, Alexander Hamilton became Secretary of the Treasury. His public duties had kept him from taking an active part as a director of the Bank of New York after the first two years of the bank's existence, but he continued to show a lively interest in its welfare, and he was the firm friend and adviser of its cashier, William Seton. In 1790 the bank was made the agent of the United States for the sale of 200,000 guilders. In the same year Hamilton laid before Congress a plan for the establishment of a great national bank. It was received with much favor, and on the 19th of February, 1791, the Bank of the United States went into operation.

In November of the same year, a letter was addressed to the president and directors of the Bank of the United States by the officers of the Bank of New York, offering to them three hundred shares of the new stock of the bank at par. The offer was declined, as the directors of the Bank of the United States did not feel authorized to invest in the stock of the state banks.

Arrangements had been made by the directors of the Bank of the United States to establish a branch of that institution in the city of New York. The plan seems not to have met the approval of Hamilton, and under date of November 25, 1791, he wrote to William Seton.—

"I seize the first moment of leisure to answer your letter of the 21st inst. Strange as it may appear to you, it is not more strange than true that the whole affair of branches was *begun*, *continued*, and *ended*, not only without my participation, but *against my judgment.*

"When I say against my judgment, you will not understand that my opinion was given and overruled, for I never was consulted; but that the steps taken were contrary to my private opinion of the course which ought to have been pursued.

"I am sensible of the inconveniences to be apprehended, and I regret them, but I do not know that it will be in my power to avert them.

"Ultimately, it will be incumbent on me to place the public funds in the keeping of the branch; but it *may be depended upon* that I shall *precipitate nothing*, but shall so conduct the transfer as not to embarrass or disturb your institution. I have not time to say more at present, except that, if there are *finally* to be two institutions, my regard for you makes me wish you may feel yourself at liberty to take your fortune with the branch which must preponderate."

Hamilton had evidently hoped to make the Bank of New York the exclusive agent of the United States government in New York. In January, 1791, he had written to Mr. Seton:-

"I feel great satisfaction in knowing from yourself that your institution rejects the idea of a coalition with the new project, or rather hydra of projects.

"I shall labor to give what has taken place a turn favorable to another union, the propriety of which is, as you say, clearly illustrated by the present state of things. It is my wish that the Bank of New York may, by all means, continue to receive deposits from the collector, in the paper of the Bank of the United States, and that they may also receive payment for the Dutch bills in the same paper. This paper may either be remitted to the treasurer or remain in the bank, as itself shall deem most expedient. I have explicitly directed the treasurer to forbear drawing on the Bank of New York, without special direction from me. And my intention is to leave you in possession of all the money you have or may receive till I am assured that the present storm is effectually weathered.

"Everybody here sees the propriety of your having refused the paper of the Bank of the United States in such a crisis of your affairs. Be confidential with me; if you are pressed, whatever support may be in my power shall be afforded. I consider the public interest as materially involved in aiding a valuable institution like yours to withstand the attacks of a confederated host of frantic and, I fear, in too many instances, unprincipled gamblers.

"Adieu. Heaven take care of good men and good views!"

The proposed plan was carried out, however, and a branch of the national institution called the "Office of Discount and Deposit" was established in New York. On the 20th of March, 1792, a committee was appointed on the part of the Bank of the United States, to meet and confer with the directors of the Bank of New York upon the best means of promoting a friendly intercourse between the two institutions. A conference was accordingly held, which resulted in a formal correspondence, expressing a desire and willingness on the part of each institution to coöperate in any measure calculated to inspire mutual confidence or public accommodation.

The success of the Bank of New York was so marked that early in 1791 a rival institution was projected. Hamilton heard of the scheme and was not slow in expressing his views regarding it. In a letter to William Seton, under date of January 18, 1791, he wrote:—

"I have learnt with infinite pain the circumstance of a new bank having started up in your city. Its effects cannot but be in every way pernicious. These extravagant sallies of speculation do injury to the government, and to the whole system of public credit, by disgusting all sober citizens, and giving a wild air to everything. 'T is impossible but that three great banks in one city must raise such a mass of artificial credit as must endanger every one of them, and do harm in every view.

"I sincerely hope that the Bank of New York will listen to no coalition with this newly engendered monster; a better alliance, I am strongly persuaded, will be brought about for it, and the joint force of two solid institutions will, without effort or violence, remove the excrescence which has just appeared, and which I consider as a dangerous tumor in your political and commercial economy.

"I express myself in these *strong terms* to you confidentially, not that I have any objection to my opinion being known as to the nature and tendency of the thing."

At the next session of the Legislature, in February, 1792, an attempt to obtain a charter for the proposed bank was made. Two petitions for an act of incorporation were at first presented by different persons;

one for an institution to be called the Million Bank, and another for one to be called the State Bank. The projectors of the first scheme, however, finally withdrew in favor of the latter. A committee to whom the subject was referred reported that, as the proposed plan contained certain propositions for opening canals and furthering the agricultural and commercial interests of the State, it merited the serious attention of the Legislature, and leave was asked to bring in a bill. A bill to incorporate the subscribers to the State Bank was afterward read for the first time, and referred again to the committee. No further report was made upon it during the session, and the scheme thus proved abortive.

During the session of the Legislature in 1792, the president and directors of the Bank of New York signified to that body their willingness to receive from the state treasurer any of the money belonging to the State which it was proposed to lend to individuals or bodies corporate, and to pay not above six per cent. interest therefor, the loan to be payable upon three months' notice. The projectors of the rival institution also proposed to the Legislature to take the state funds individually as a loan at seven per cent. on security of the funded debt of the United States, "unless the State would prefer investing the money in the new bank which is to be established, or lending it in small sums upon mortgages of real estate."

The Legislature subsequently passed an act authorizing the state treasurer to deposit in the Bank of New York certificates for the funded debt of the United States to the amount of nearly two million dollars; the bank agreeing to collect the interest on the same, and pay it over to the treasurer without charge. In conformity with this act, Gerard Bancker, treasurer of the State, was elected a director of the bank on the 24th of May, 1792.

In 1791 there was a mania for speculation in the principal cities, and during August of that year United States Bank scrip sold for 195. In September it fell to 110, but rallied to 145. Several failures were the result, the public credit suffered, and the six per cent. issues of the United States were depressed. The Secretary of the Treasury accordingly authorized the cashier of the Bank of New York to buy government bonds in small lots to relieve the merchants and sustain the credit of the United States. This had the desired effect for a time, but the relief proved to be merely temporary. By March of the following year the distress had increased until it amounted almost to a panic, and the Secretary of the Treasury was prompted to come again to the rescue of the mercantile community. On the 25th of March, 1792, he wrote to the cashier of the Bank of New York, authorizing him to purchase United States stocks at par to the amount of fifty thousand dollars.

"It will be very probably conjectured," he wrote, "that you appear for the public, and the conjecture may be left to have its course, but without confession. The purchase ought, in the present state of things, to be at auction, and not till to-morrow evening. But if the purchase at auction will not tend as well to the purpose of relief as a different mode, it may be departed from; the usual note must be made of persons, time, etc. You will consider whether done all at once, or a part now and a part then, will best answer the purpose. In the state of this market, the latter mode is found preferable. I have just received a letter from Mr. Short, our minister resident, dated Amsterdam, 28th December, by which he informs me that he has effected a loan for three millions of florins at four per cent. interest, on account of the United States. This may be announced; and as, in the present moment of suspicion, some minds may be disposed to consider the thing as a mere expedient to support the stocks, I pledge my honor for its exact truth. . . .

"While I encourage due exertion in the banks, I observe that I hope they will put nothing to risk. No calamity truly public can happen while these institutions remain sound. They must, therefore, not yield too far to the impulse of circumstances."

This letter was received on the following day, and the cashier of the bank wrote in reply, under date of March 25th: —

"We have no public sales of stocks now in the evenings; therefore I cannot go into the market till to-morrow, and although the sum is small, yet be assured it will be a relief. The collector has furnished the list of names of those who have duties to pay between this and the first of May, and our directors have given out that they will discount on a deposit of stock. The large dealers in stock are to have a meeting this evening, and, it is reported, will enter into an absolute agreement not to draw out any specie from the banks for three months to come — so that from to-morrow I hope the prospect will brighten. I have made as public as possible the new loan obtained in Amsterdam; it gives most universal satisfaction."

The financial trouble seems to have increased in intensity; and on the 4th of April the Secretary wrote to Mr. Seton, saying that he was pained beyond expression at the accounts he had received of the financial distress of his fellow-citizens, and authorizing him to apply $50,000 additional to purchases of stock at such times as might be thought most beneficial to the public. On the 12th of April the Secretary wrote again to Mr. Seton, giving him additional latitude in the purchase of the six per cents. and the deferred stock. He also wrote to the directors of the bank, confirming his previous instructions to Mr. Seton, and adding $50,000 more to the amount already appropriated for the relief of the merchants; making in all $150,000.

Mr. Seton's reply, under date of April 16th, shows the beneficial effect of this welcome aid:—

"I received your letter by the express, on Friday morning, previous to which I had been relieving a few by purchases of stock, upon the strength of the second extension of fifty thousand dollars. At noon I went into the market, but the applications were so numerous, and so vastly beyond my expectations, I found it necessary to declare I could take but very small sums from each. However, notwithstanding this, every one pressed forward, and was so eager that I could only take down names upon a declaration that I would average the whole. This I did, that no one might be left without some relief; so that the investment of one hundred thousand dollars goes to upwards of eighty persons, from which you may form a judgment that your orders for purchases were well timed. At the same time, it is an evidence of the great and universal distress which prevails, and which I am sorry to say is such that it would be utterly impossible to make purchases equal to the relief. However, it cannot now be worse; and when the public mind cools down a little, it is to be hoped that good will arise out of the evil, that the spirit of industry instead of gambling will revive, and that the stocks will come to their proper and real value."

The judicious course of the Secretary seems to have had the desired result, and the relief that these timely purchases of stock by the Treasury Department afforded to a community which had been almost drained of its specie as a result of excessive importations can hardly be estimated at the present day.[1]

In 1792 the Society for Establishing Useful Manufactures, in which Alexander Hamilton was interested, and which had recently been organized in Philadelphia,

[1] A similar service has lately been rendered by the bank to the business public. On the 16th of May, 1884, at the height of the excitement and alarm which followed the failure of the Marine Bank and of Grant & Ward, the Bank of New York made loans upon United States stocks during the day, amounting to $4,000,000. This, in a measure, relieved the financial stringency and averted a panic which, if unchecked, would have resulted in the closing of the Stock Exchange and in general disaster.

applied to the Bank of New York for a loan to enable it to carry out its plans for building factories at Paterson, N. J. The busy city which to-day has 60,000 inhabitants was then a settlement with ten dwellings. At Hamilton's suggestion the bank lent to the society $10,000 on pledge of United States deferred stock, with interest at five per cent., and a few months later a further loan of $35,000 was made to the society on similar terms. In his letter to Mr. Seton on the subject Hamilton said: "I will add more, that in my opinion banks ought to afford accommodation in such cases upon easy terms of interest. I think five per cent. ought to suffice, for a direct public good is presented. And institutions of this kind, within reasonable limits, ought to consider it as a principal object to promote public purposes."

In Mr. Seton's reply on the 25th of June he indicated the feelings of the officers of the bank toward Hamilton. "Our directors are informed of your sentiments respecting the loan to the Manufacturing Society. Be assured, my dear sir, that they have so much confidence in any measure pointed out by you, and take so much pleasure in promoting your views, which they are well convinced are ever intended for the public good, that by complying with your wishes they are glad to have an opportunity of retaliating the obligations this institution is under to you."

At the annual meeting in June, 1794, William Seton

Cashier of the Bank,

Pay to the Bearer John Burk [illegible] Hundred and twenty four Dollars 24/96

New-York, the 24 Day of August 1784

Aaron Burr

---

Cashier of the Bank,

Pay to ——— or Bearer,

four thousand pounds ——— Paper.

New-York, the 2 — Day of April 1789

£.14

[illegible]

---

Cashier of the Bank of *New-York*,

Pay to M. de beaumez ——— or Bearer,

——— twenty five ——— Dollars.

New-York, the 2[illegible] Day of [illegible] 1795

[illegible] talleyrand

sent in his resignation as cashier of the bank, and Charles Wilkes was chosen in his stead. Mr. Seton had been connected with the bank since its organization, and had proved to be a faithful and efficient officer. His correspondence with Alexander Hamilton in connection with the bank shows the regard which that eminent man felt for him and the confidence he placed in his judgment and integrity. Mr. Seton died in 1798 at the age of fifty-two.

In October, 1793, Richard Varick, mayor of the city of New York, presented a resolution of the common council asking for a loan of $5000, "to aid the poor and most distressed citizens of Philadelphia, under the pressure of their present great calamity;" to which proposition the board of directors agreed, taking as security a corporation bond.

The Bank of New York was able to extend efficient aid to the national government during 1794. On the 6th of October, in response to the application of the Secretary of the Treasury, a loan of $200,000 was made to the United States for four months at five per cent. An agreement was made in January, 1795, to continue this loan for eight months from its maturity, and it was subsequently renewed for another year.

On the 9th of December, 1794, the president presented at the directors' meeting a letter from the Secretary of the Treasury requesting a loan of $100,000 for one year at five per cent. interest, with the privilege of annual renewals for five years. The loan was for the purpose of redeeming a part of the debt of the United States. A similar letter was sent to banks in other cities, and the directors of the Bank of New York promptly acquiesced in the plan. In acknowledging the acceptance of his proposition by the bank, Hamilton said: "It gives me pleasure to have this fresh opportunity of bearing testimony to the liberal and patriotic zeal for the service of the United States which the Bank of New York has on every occasion evinced."

The Secretary of the Treasury again asked for a loan in August, 1795. The sum of $120,000 was required for six months, and it was also requested that the loan of $200,000, which would mature on the 8th of October, should be continued to the 8th of April following. Both loans, it was proposed, should bear interest at the rate of six per cent., and should be secured by the same amount of six per cent. stock, the bank to have the privilege of selling the stock at the market price on the maturity of the loans if there should be a default in the payment thereof. These requests were promptly granted.

# CHAPTER V

## 1796–1811

*Change of Location of the Bank. — The New Building in Wall Street. — Purchase of United States Stock from the State in 1797. — Aid rendered to the State in 1797. — The Yellow Fever of 1798. — Temporary Removal of the Bank to Greenwich in 1799. — Incorporation of the Manhattan Company in 1799. — Action of the Bank thereupon. — Death of Gulian Verplanck and Election of Nicholas Gouverneur as President in 1799. — Petition to the Legislature for Alterations in Charter in 1801. — Death of Nicholas Gouverneur and Election of Herman Le Roy as President in 1802. — Proposal of the City Government with Reference to the Charter of the Bank. — Resignation of Herman Le Roy and Election of Matthew Clarkson as President in 1804. — Extension of the Charter by the Legislature in 1808. — Loans to the State by the Bank. — Petition of the Bank to the Legislature respecting the Bank of the United States.*

THE business of the bank had in 1796 so increased that better facilities and a more desirable location were needed for it. Accordingly, in November of that year, the house and lot on the corner of Wall and William streets were bought of Mr. William Constable for eleven thousand pounds, New York currency. In April following, it was decided to tear down the house that stood on the lot, and to erect a building with the necessary vaults for the business of the bank. Messrs. Richard Varick, John B. Coles, and Nicholas Gouverneur were appointed a committee to make the necessary contracts and superintend the construction of the building.

The corner-stone of the new structure was laid with appropriate ceremonies on the 22d of June, 1797, by Gulian Verplanck, president of the bank, and George Doolet, the architect, in presence of the directors and a large assemblage of citizens. On Monday, the 23d of April of the following year, the cash and books were removed to the new quarters, and business was begun that day. The house of Francis B. Winthrop in Wall Street was leased for eight years at an annual rent of three hundred and fifty pounds and the taxes, and was appropriated as a residence for the cashier.

No record remains of the size of the lot purchased of Mr. Constable, nor of the bank building erected thereon; but some years after, in widening William Street, seven feet were taken off that side of the building, and a new roof was thrown over the bank and over a small dwelling-house which stood immediately in the rear of it; thus forming the edifice that was so long familiar to the citizens of New York. The corporation allowed the bank $35,000 as damages; a sum which at that time was thought to be a very large allowance.

In accordance with an act passed by the Legislature to render the funds of the State more productive, a committee was appointed on the part of the bank, early in 1797, to confer with a committee appointed by the governor with reference to the purchase by the bank of certain United States stock held by the State. A part of this stock was redeemable by the United States in installments, which were not large enough at any one time to be of material aid to the state treasury. The deferred stock was irredeemable, and bore no interest until 1800. The market value of the stock was from twenty to thirty per cent. below par. An agreement was finally made that the bank should purchase $566,463.70 of the United States six per cent. stock and $799,686.51 of United States deferred stock, the whole to be paid for at its nominal value, on the second Tuesday in May, 1809, and should pay interest on the same at six per cent., providing that the interest on the deferred stock should not begin until the year 1800. The bank further agreed to advance the State from time to time such sums as should be required. The immediate benefit to the bank from this purchase was, that it was permitted to increase its indebtedness to a proportionate amount beyond the limit fixed by its act of incorporation, and further, that it became the financial depository of the State.

Another application for pecuniary aid was made by the State during the same year. In November, 1797, the president laid before the board of directors a letter from the governor, setting forth the need of the State for money to be used for its defence, and enclosing a copy of the act of the Legislature authorizing the governor to borrow $315,000 on the faith of the State for that purpose. A loan of $200,000, in addition to the loans already existing, which amounted to $128,000, was accordingly made to the State, the amount of the loan being passed to its credit, and interest at the rate of six per cent. charged on such sums as should be drawn.

The building previously occupied by the bank in Pearl Street was sold by Messrs. A. L. Bleecker & Sons, auctioneers, in January, 1798, at the Tontine Coffee House, for 10,600 pounds, New York currency. It was described in the "Daily Advertiser" of December 14, 1797, as "comprising two spacious three-story dwelling-houses under one roof; the whole in good repair, and replete with accommodations and conveniences for business, as well as for family purposes. Front on Pearl Street, fifty feet eleven inches; rear, thirty-seven feet eight inches; length on the westerly side, one hundred and ninety-two feet ten inches; on the easterly side, one hundred and eighty feet nine inches."

The yellow fever had broken out in the city during the summer of 1798. One of the clerks of the bank, a bookkeeper, fell a victim to the pestilence, and the directors presented five hundred dollars to his widow. At the close of the year a gratuity of twenty per cent. on their salaries was given to all persons in the service of the bank during the prevalence of the epidemic.

Fearing that the fever would again appear during the coming year, it was thought prudent by the directors of the bank to provide a place for transacting its business outside of the city in case of emergency. Accordingly, in the spring of 1799, the Bank of New York joined with the Branch Bank of the United States in purchasing two plots in Greenwich village for five hundred dollars each city lot, and a suitable building was erected by the bank on its lot at a cost of $8000. The plot of ground which was purchased comprised sixteen city lots, fronting on Bank, Factory (afterward Waverley Place), and Hammond streets. The property was sold in 1843 for $30,000.

The precaution of the directors proved a wise one. The fever raged with great virulence during the summer of 1799, and it became necessary to remove the bank to the building at Greenwich on the 23d of September. There the business of the bank was carried on until late in November. Notice was given in the daily papers, at the time of removal, that notes and bills intended for discount might be left for the cashier at the Tontine Tavern, in Broadway, under sealed cover, on Mondays and Wednesdays, and would be offered for discount on the following days. Also that a messenger from the bank would call at the City Tavern, in Broadway, for letters directed to the cashier, and that any article of value enclosed would be at the risk of the owner.

The Bank of New York had now been in existence for fifteen years without a rival. It had obtained its charter with great difficulty, and those interested in its success could not be expected to look with complacency upon any attempt to establish an institution to compete with it. Neither did the public desire any additional banking facilities. But suddenly and unexpectedly a formidable corporation made its appearance as a bank of deposit and issue in New York. It was the result of the craft and sagacity of Aaron Burr. A petition was presented to the Legislature in the spring of 1799, asking for a charter for a company with a capital of two millions of dollars for the purpose of introducing pure water into the city of New York. As the entire capital might not be required, a clause in the bill provided that the surplus capital might be "employed in the purchase of public or other stocks, or in any other moneyed transactions or operations not inconsistent with the laws and constitution of the State of New York." In these words the real purpose of the scheme was concealed.

The prevalence of the yellow fever during the previous summer had created an alarm which made the passage of a bill to improve the sanitary condition of New York an easy matter. Toward the end of the session the bill incorporating the Manhattan Company was accordingly passed by the Legislature, and passed without a suspicion on the part of the majority of those who voted for it that it contained a grant of banking privileges. But the real purpose of the scheme was soon made manifest. The discovery created great excitement and indignation. It was charged that the Legislature had been cheated so as to enable Burr and his friends to control a majority of the stock of the company and use its capital for their own purposes.

The plans of the persons interested were speedily carried out, and notice was given that the banking operations of the company would commence in September with a capital of $500,000.

A special meeting of the directors of the Bank of New York was called by the president on the 22d of August to consider the propriety of taking the notes which might be issued by the Manhattan Company, and it was resolved that such notes should not be taken. But upon further consideration it was thought best to adopt a different policy, and on the 15th of April, 1800, the resolution was rescinded.

The sudden death of Gulian Verplanck, on the 20th of November, 1799, deprived the bank of the services of the distinguished citizen who had been its president during the past eight years. Mr. Verplanck was the son of Gulian Verplanck, a prominent merchant of New York, and was born February 11, 1751. On his father's side he was descended from a Dutch family that came to this country from Holland in the time of Governor Stuyvesant; by his mother he was of French

Huguenot extraction, and he inherited many characteristics of each of these races. Being but nine months old when his father died, he was taken care of by his brother Samuel, who was an importer and banker, and one of the twenty-four founders of the New York Chamber of Commerce in 1768. After his graduation at Kings (now Columbia) College in the class with Bishop Moore and Gouverneur Morris, he was sent to Europe to receive a mercantile training under his uncle, Daniel Crommelin, then a member of the great banking and commercial house of Daniel Crommelin & Sons of Amsterdam. After his return to New York Mr. Verplanck soon became a prominent citizen. He was a highly accomplished and fluent orator, and as early as 1788 he was a representative in the Assembly of the State. In 1791 he was elected speaker, and again in 1796, and he was also one of the regents of the University of the State. He was president of the Bank of New York from 1791 until his death, in 1799.

At the meeting of the directors on the 7th of December, 1799, Nicholas Gouverneur was elected president, to fill the vacancy caused by the death of Mr. Verplanck.

The aid and accommodation which the bank had rendered in the fiscal operations of the United States and the State of New York now seemed to justify its directors in asking for some legislative action in its behalf. In February, 1801, a petition was presented to

Gulian Verplanck

PRESIDENT 1791-1799

the Legislature by the directors, asking that the limitation to the charter be rescinded (the charter granted to the Manhattan Company being perpetual); that the clause should be repealed which provided that four of the directors elected in any one year should be ineligible for one year after their term of office had expired; and that the clauses limiting the amount of property which the bank might hold, and prohibiting the bank from dealing in any species of stock that might be created under the act of the United States, or of any particular State, should also be repealed.

This petition was presented by Mr. Deming, who, at the request of the board of directors, urged upon the Legislature the justice of allowing the bank to pay a part of its indebtedness to the State in the bills of credit issued by the State. These, to the amount of $103,000, being unsalable, had for a long time been in the possession of the bank. As the result of this petition, the Legislature amended the act of incorporation so far as it affected the ineligibility of directors, and also made it lawful for the treasurer of the State to receive from the bank the bills of credit referred to.

At the meeting of the directors on the 16th of July, 1802, the death of Nicholas Gouverneur, the president of the bank, was announced. Mr. Gouverneur succeeded Gulian Verplanck as president upon the death of that gentleman in 1799. On the 29th of July

Herman Le Roy was elected to fill the vacancy in place of Mr. Gouverneur.

The Bank of New York was now enjoying a season of prosperity in common with the other institutions of the kind that had sprung up since its organization. The number of banks in the country had greatly increased. By 1803 it was estimated that there were upwards of forty in active operation. Business throughout the country had received an immense impetus, and the outlook for the future was promising. Under these circumstances the city government thought it desirable to share, if possible, in the prosperity of the Bank of New York. At a meeting of the directors of the bank in February, 1803, a letter was read from Edward Livingston, mayor of the city, in which he requested the opinion of the board as to the expediency of having the term of the charter of the bank extended, and its capital increased by one million dollars. The dividends on the new capital, he proposed, should be subject to a deduction of two per cent. on the amount of that capital, which sum should be appropriated to the use of the corporation. The board of directors did not approve of the proposition.

From an early period in its history the Bank of New York has been preëminently a merchants' bank, and has for a long series of years made advances on merchandise. In 1804 this was made a special branch of its business, and John Ellis was appointed on the part of the bank to inspect and appraise the goods offered as security for loans. For this duty he received a commission of one half of one per cent. of the loan; the commission to be paid by the borrower.

In June, 1804, Herman Le Roy resigned the office of president of the bank, and was succeeded by Matthew Clarkson. Herman Le Roy was the son of Jacob Le Roy, the head of the well-known firm of Jacob Le Roy & Sons. He was born in New York in 1758, and, while a youth, was sent to Holland to receive a commercial education. After his return to this country he founded the house of Le Roy, Bayard & Co., which afterward, under the style of Le Roy, Bayard & McEvers, became the most important commercial establishment in the United States. Mr. Le Roy died at his house, No. 7 Greenwich Street, March 31, 1841.

In April, 1808, the Legislature of the State passed an act extending the charter of the bank (which would expire by limitation on the second Tuesday in May, 1811) to the second Tuesday in May, 1820. The act further provided that the comptroller of the State should no longer be *ex officio* a director of the bank, but that the governor should appoint, on behalf of the State, two directors residing in the city of New York; who should not be directors in any other bank, and that the State should not be entitled to vote at any election of directors. During the same month the comptroller of the State, having notified the bank that he was authorized by a recent act of the Legislature to borrow from the city banks $450,000 on the credit of the State, and possibly $150,000 more, the bank advanced $200,000 of the amount required.

On the 13th of April of the same year, an additional loan of $150,000 was made to the State at the request of the comptroller.

The credit of the United States had become so well established in 1809, that in April of that year the bank was able to sell $100,000 of the United States stock bought of the State in 1797, at 102. Another sale was made of $21,000 in May at the same price, and in October $200,000 was sold at 104.

In January, 1810, a memorial and petition presented by the bank to the Legislature showed that in 1797 the bank purchased at par from the State $1,390,871.50 of United States stock, then at a discount of from fifteen to twenty per cent., and that the bank had paid on account of the purchase $103,908, and had lent to the State $460,000. The bank requested that the payment of the balance due might be postponed to the year 1818. An act was accordingly passed by the Legislature, extending the time of payment, as desired, to the second Tuesday in May, 1818, on condition that the bank should, if required, make loans to the State not to exceed $250,000 in amount.

The charter of the Bank of the United States expired

Herman LeRoy

PRESIDENT 1802-1804

in 1811, and great fears were entertained that a severe crisis must follow the winding up of its affairs. Strenuous efforts were made by its friends to obtain a renewal of the charter, and these met with vigorous opposition. The directors of the Bank of New York felt it to be their duty to express their views on the subject, and in January, 1811, they prepared a memorial to be presented to Congress, asking for a renewal of the charter. In it they stated that they regarded the institution of the Bank of the United States as highly useful to the state banks. From the extent of its capital, its numerous branches in every part of the United States, and, above all, from the protection of the government, which it enjoyed, it was enabled, they believed, to equalize the balance of specie capital among the different cities, and, in case of any sudden pressure upon the merchants, to step forward to their aid in a degree which the state institutions were unable to do. The directors further stated that, as the Bank of New York had been established prior to the incorporation of the Bank of the United States, they had witnessed from the commencement of the branch bank in the city of New York the influence of such an institution, as well as the conduct of those to whom its management had been confided during the whole period; and they declared with confidence that the power had been uniformly exerted with prudence as it respected the public, and with great liberality as it respected the other banks.

The inconvenience and danger to the public which would attend the withdrawal of so considerable a part of the active capital of a commercial community were dwelt upon in the memorial, and other reasons given for renewing the charter of the bank; but as the efforts to that end proved fruitless, the only effect of the memorial was to show the friendly feeling of the Bank of New York toward other banking institutions.

FIVE
FIVE
TWO
TWO
2
of the BANK of NEW YORK

# CHAPTER VI

## 1812–1824

*Increase of the Capital by Legislative Enactment authorizing Subscriptions for the Stock by Hamilton and Union Colleges in 1813. — Financial Aid rendered the Government during the War of 1812. — Suspension of Specie Payments in 1814. — Condition of the Bank of New York at the Time. — Action of the Secretary of the Treasury respecting Treasury Notes. — Efforts to resume Specie Payments. — Final Resumption in 1817. — Loan to the North River Steamboat Company. — Temporary Removal of the Bank to Greenwich in 1822. — Loan of £200,000 effected in London in 1822. — Payment of Amount due the State in 1823.*

IN April, 1813, an act was passed by the Legislature, extending the charter of certain banks to the first Tuesday of June, 1832. Among these was the Bank of New York. A provision of the act authorized the treasurers of several colleges to subscribe for a certain amount of stock of the different banks at the price paid by the original stockholders, the capital of each bank to be increased accordingly. Under this authority Union College was entitled to $20,000 of the capital stock of the Bank of New York, Hamilton College to $15,000, and the Common-School Fund to $15,000 of stock, the amount of $50,000 being added to the capital of the bank. This made the total capital $950,000.

The trustees of Hamilton College sold to the bank,

in August, 1813, their right of subscription, at the rate of $126 per share. As the trustees of Union College were not willing to accept the market price for the stock to which they were entitled, the directors of the bank borrowed of Peter P. Goelet, one of their number, forty shares of stock, and delivered the certificates to the trustees. The stock was subsequently bought of the trustees by the bank.

When war was declared with Great Britain in 1812, and it became necessary for the general government as well as the State and city to ask for financial aid, the Bank of New York was prompt in responding to the calls upon it. On the 2d of November, 1813, the bank opened subscription books for the loan of sixteen millions asked for by the Secretary of the Treasury, to meet the expenditures of the war. In September, 1814, it made a loan to the State of $20,000, and also a loan of $100,000 to the corporation for the defence of the city.

On the 8th of December, 1814, the Secretary of War, through Governor Tompkins, requested a loan of $100,000, to be secured by treasury notes. The directors decided that it was inexpedient to make such a loan, but expressed a willingness to make an additional loan to the city, if the security of the corporation was given for the repayment thereof, or to the State of an amount equal to the debt of the bank to the State, which would not be due until 1818. In

August, 1814, two hundred and fifty dollars was sent to the Committee of Defence then organized in the city, as a contribution toward the expense of erecting fortifications. On the 24th of June, the directors, in reply to an inquiry of the comptroller of the State as to how large a loan the bank would make to the State, offered to lend such amount as might be required, not exceeding the amount due the State, or to anticipate the payment of its indebtedness amounting to $435,406.47.

The war of 1812 caused a great deal of commercial distress, which was increased by the withdrawal of the facilities of the United States Bank, the charter of which had expired. The necessity of limiting credits led to a general distrust, which might have produced a panic but for the prompt action of the banks. Several meetings had been held by the banks of Philadelphia, where the distress was greater, on account of the winding up of the United States Bank; and on the 20th of August, committees from the Manhattan Company, the Mechanics', and the City Bank extended an invitation to the other banks in New York to appoint committees to meet with them at the Manhattan Company's bank at 6 P. M. on the 22d inst. to consider the state of the banks and of commercial credit, and to take such measures as might be advisable for the relief of the merchants of this city. The president and cashier were appointed as a committee for the Bank of New York, with authority to pledge the coöperation of the bank in such measures as might be adopted by the unanimous consent of the banks. No record exists of what was done at this meeting; but at a meeting of the committees representing the banks, held on the 21st of August, letters were read from the cashiers of several of the Philadelphia banks, stating that it had been decided to suspend specie payments in that city. It was thereupon voted that a similar course on the part of the New York banks was unavoidable, and this opinion being afterward indorsed by all of the banks, specie payments were accordingly suspended.

A statement, showing the condition of the Bank of New York at the time of the suspension of specie payments, September 1, 1814, was made to the comptroller of the State, and copies were sent to the register of the Court of Chancery, and also to Messrs. Gordon S. Mumford and Samuel A. Lawrence, directors appointed by the State, to be forwarded to the governor.

LIABILITIES.

| | | |
|---|---|---|
| Capital | | $965,000 00 |
| Profits | | 139,506 53 |
| Due the State of New York | $1,262,091 47 | |
| Less Loans to State | 806,685 00 | |
| | | 455,406 47 |
| Notes in circulation, including post-notes and all notes ever issued, none having been carried to account as lost since 1784 | | 533,800 00 |
| Due on deposits | | 983,986 00 |
| | | $3,077,699 00 |

ASSETS.

| | |
|---|---|
| Due the bank on notes and bills discounted | $2,341,190 00 |
| Due the bank on all other loans . . . . . | 148,345 00 |
| Specie in the vaults and in Albany . . . . | 300,912 00 |
| Due from Bank of North America, Philadelphia . . . . . . . . . . . . | 112,580 00 |
| Due from Massachusetts Bank, Boston . . | 29,899 00 |
| Due from city banks . . . . . . . . | 35,528 00 |
| Houses and lots in New York, cost $104,695, now estimated as . . . . . . . . | 74,695 00 |
| Interest due on loans . . . . . . . . | 34,550 00 |
| | [1] $3,077,699 00 |

That the wants of the United States Treasury were great at this time may be inferred from the fact that in

[1] A comparison of these figures with the condensed statement of the bank made to the comptroller of the currency, in October, 1883, will illustrate the growth of its business since the War of 1812: —

LIABILITIES.

| | |
|---|---|
| Capital stock . . . . . . . . . . . . . | $2,000,000 00 |
| Surplus, with profit and loss account . . . . . . | 1,042,978 29 |
| Circulation . . . . . . . . . . . . . | 450,000 00 |
| Dividends not called for . . . . . . . . . | 10,048 60 |
| Due depositors, correspondents, and certified checks . | 13,370,930 51 |
| | $16,873,957 40 |

RESOURCES.

| | |
|---|---|
| Loans and discounts . . . . . . . . . . | $8,244,551 43 |
| United States and other bonds and stocks . . . . | 524,348 05 |
| Real estate . . . . . . . . . . . . | 250,000 00 |
| Checks and cash items . . . . . . . . . . | 5,898,057 92 |
| Specie and legal tender notes . . . . . . . . | 1,934,500 00 |
| Due from United States Treasury . . . . . . . | 22,500 00 |
| | $16,873,957 40 |

December, 1814, the Secretary of War asked, through Governor Tompkins, for a loan of $100,000 for a short period, secured by treasury notes. The treasury notes were at that time generally discredited by the banks.

In January, 1815, the Secretary of the Treasury issued a circular to the banks, notifying them that instructions had been issued to all collectors and other receivers of the United States to refuse to receive the notes of banks which did not pay their notes on demand in gold or silver, or which, having suspended specie payments, should not receive treasury notes at par and reissue them in payment of all demands on the banks to such persons as should choose to receive them. The Secretary further requested a distinct answer from each bank as to whether it would agree to receive, issue, and circulate treasury notes, and whether, if it declined to do so, the bank paid its notes in gold or silver. If a bank declined to make such agreement, its notes would not be received by the United States.

The cashier of the Bank of New York was directed to inform the Treasury Department that the bank declined to enter into any agreement to receive treasury notes in the manner proposed.

Peace with England was ratified in 1815, and business immediately began to revive. Importations were immense, and soon gave the government a large surplus revenue. It was deemed expedient on the part of the banks of the country to take some steps toward resuming specie payments; and the general committee of the New York banks passed a series of resolutions advising a reduction of loans, as a preparation for resumption on the first day of July, 1817, and requesting the coöperation of the banks in Philadelphia and Baltimore.

In July, 1816, a circular letter was sent by the Treasury Department to the banks, proposing that after the first day of October following, the banks should pay all notes of five dollars and under in specie. A convention of delegates from the banks throughout the country was held to consider the proposition. It was unanimously decided that as the new Bank of the United States, which had been chartered, and its branches, would not be in operation at an earlier period than the first of July following, and as it was desirable that the payment of specie by the banks should be as nearly as possible simultaneous on the part of the state banks and the Bank of the United States and its branches, the banks should resume payments in specie on the first Monday in July following. A committee was also appointed to wait upon the Secretary of the Treasury and inform him that in the judgment of the convention it was impracticable for the state banks to comply with his proposition.

This decision did not meet the views of the national or state governments. Congress resolved that after

February 20, 1817, only specie, treasury notes, and notes of specie-paying banks ought to be taken by the national treasury. A law was passed by the Legislature of New York imposing twelve per cent. interest on all notes not redeemed. In January, 1817, the convention of the banks of New York, Philadelphia, Baltimore, and Virginia met again in Philadelphia, and propositions were made by the committee representing the Bank of the United States to aid in facilitating resumption at an earlier date than was at first decided upon. These were that the Bank of the United States should discount good paper, which should be offered in New York to the amount of $2,000,000; an equal amount in Philadelphia; $1,500,000 in Baltimore; and $500,000 in Virginia. These propositions were accepted by the general committee, and ratified by the banks of New York on the 6th of February. Specie payments were accordingly resumed by the banks in the different cities on the 20th of February, 1817.

In May, 1818, the comptroller of the State having asked for proposals for a loan of $1,000,000 at six per cent., the cashier of the bank was authorized to bid for the loan at a premium not to exceed one per cent., and to bid two per cent. premium for $50,000. To redeem this loan the State appropriated and pledged four hundred thousand acres of state land, and also the balance due from the Bank of New York to the State, which then amounted to $435,000; the time of payment of this sum being extended by the act authorizing the loan to July 1, 1823.

The bid of the Bank of New York was not successful, as the entire amount was awarded to the Manhattan Company at one and one quarter per cent. premium.

On the 12th of June, 1821, the bank lent the North River Steamboat Company $55,000 for six months. The three boats of the company, the Fire Fly, the Chancellor, and the Richmond, were pledged as security, and the loan was to be paid by monthly installments; the company agreeing to suspend dividends until the loan was paid.

In August, 1822, the bank again removed its business to Greenwich on account of the epidemic then prevailing in the city. This seems to have been the last time that such a course was deemed necessary.

The debt due from the bank to the State of New York for the funded six per cent. stock of the United States, purchased from the State in 1797, was originally payable in 1809; but when the charter of the bank was renewed, the time of payment of the debt was extended until 1832. At several periods during the war, and afterward, the bank had proposed to pay off the debt; but it had always happened that these offers were made when the State, having extended the time of payment, had the power of refusal; and the offers of the bank were always declined. In fact, for various reasons it had been the desire of the successive persons who managed the finances of the State to leave the money in the custody of the bank; and this was the case when the State was borrowing money elsewhere at the rate of seven per cent.

The bank had the right to pay this debt in 1823; and in 1822 it was proposed to borrow 200,000 pounds sterling in London at five per cent., for the purpose of so doing. Mr. Wilkes, the cashier, was accordingly sent to London, after some preliminary correspondence had been had with Messrs. Baring Bros. & Co. on the subject, with full power to negotiate the loan. He sailed from New York in December, 1822, and on reaching London found the condition of the money market not favorable for the negotiation. On the 22d of July, a letter was read from him to the directors, wishing to know if it was still deemed expedient to obtain the loan. A reply was sent to him to the effect that he might spend the winter in London, if by so doing he could conduct the negotiation to the better advantage of the bank. He succeeded, however, in effecting an arrangement with Messrs. Baring Bros. & Co. for a loan, subject to the approval of the directors of the bank, and reached New York in December. The proposals of Messrs. Baring Bros. & Co. were accepted. Two hundred thousand pounds was borrowed at five per cent. per annum for eight years, and one hundred and seventy certificates of indebtedness, varying in amount from £500 to £4000, were given therefor.

Negotiations with the State were then begun, looking to an extension of the charter of the bank for fifteen years, and a continuance of a portion of the indebtedness to the State on the part of the bank. A bill embracing these propositions was introduced in the Legislature, and after passing the Assembly almost unanimously, was lost in the Senate by the casting vote of the lieutenant-governor. The debt to the State was therefore paid at maturity in 1823.

# CHAPTER VII

## 1825–1851

*Resignation of General Matthew Clarkson and Election of Charles Wilkes as President in 1825. — Loans to the Morris Canal and Banking Company in 1827 and 1829. — Proposition of Amos Kendall in Behalf of the Secretary of the Treasury to make the Bank an Agent of the Treasury in 1832. — Resignation of Charles Wilkes and Election of Cornelius Heyer as President in 1832. — Petition for an Increase of Capital in 1835. — Financial Difficulties in 1836. — A Loan of £112,500 effected in London in 1836. — Purchase of Stock from the State in 1837. — Suspension of Specie Payments in 1837. — Resumption in 1838. — Difficulties of the Philadelphia Banks. — Financial Aid to the State in 1840. — Death of Cornelius Heyer. — Election of John Oothout as President in 1843. — Death of Joshua Waddington.*

ON the 13th of April, 1825, General Matthew Clarkson resigned the office of president. At the meeting of directors on the 19th, his resignation was reluctantly accepted, and the board passed a series of resolutions expressing the grateful thanks of the institution for the disinterested services rendered by him during the twenty-one years he had so acceptably filled the office of president.

General Matthew Clarkson was born on the 17th of October, 1758, in the city of New York, where his immediate ancestors had held high and confidential civil offices and filled them with fidelity and ability.

His family were originally from Yorkshire, England, in which country they had lived for many generations.

At the age of seventeen he entered the army of the United States, during the War of Independence, and served successfully on the staff of Arnold and on that of Lincoln, with the rank of major. Few officers were as often in the face of the enemy, and on such memorable occasions, as Clarkson. As he participated in two of the greatest reverses of the Americans, — the defeat on Long Island and the fall of Charleston, — so he was engaged in two of their most brilliant achievements, — the capitulation of General Burgoyne and of Lord Cornwallis.

At the close of the war he retired to civil life, though he was a general officer in the militia for more than fourteen years. He manifested a deep interest in the politics of the commonwealth, and was elected to both houses of the state legislature. A Federalist in his principles, and associated with Hamilton, Jay, and others, he exercised his personal influence in the support of such men and measures as in his view were identified with the happiness and prosperity of the country.

For a time he was engaged in business with John Vanderbilt, under the firm name of Vanderbilt & Clarkson. After a successful partnership his mercantile relations with Mr. Vanderbilt were dissolved; and, conducting business for a short time on his own account, he at length became associated in his brother's firm, which was known as S. & L. Clarkson & Co.

Several positions of emolument and honor were, at different times, offered to General Clarkson, among others the collectorship of the port of New York, but they were all declined.

General Clarkson died on the 25th of April, 1825; but a few days after his resignation. The last years of his life were principally devoted to the promotion of those institutions which reflect so much honor on the religion, the education, and the benevolence of this country. Chancellor Kent said of him, that "it was his business and his delight to afford consolation to the distressed, to relieve the wants of the needy, to instruct the ignorant, to reclaim the vicious, to visit the fatherless and the widow in their affliction, and to keep himself unspotted from the world." And the Hon. De Witt Clinton, the governor, in a memorial address, said: "As long as benevolence is respected among men, as long as piety is held in veneration, so long will the name of Clarkson be ranked among the excellent men who have illustrated in their lives the greatness of goodness."

On the 12th of May, 1825, Charles Wilkes was elected to the office of president, made vacant by the resignation of Mr. Clarkson.

The Morris Canal and Banking Company of New Jersey applied to the bank in June, 1827, requesting a

MATTHEW CLARKSON.

*Original by S L Waldo, in the possession of Mrs David Clarkson*

*1823 Æt 64*

subscription of $300,000 to a loan which it wished to obtain, and which was to be repaid by the proceeds of the sale of 3000 shares of the canal company's stock. The subscribers to the loan were to receive post-notes payable in two years with interest at six per cent., payable quarterly, and the canal company was to give as security for said post-notes a judgment to Charles Wilkes, Jacob Lorillard, and Isaac Wright, trustees. The directors of the bank agreed to subscribe to $25,000 of the loan, the subscription to be binding when $200,000 had been subscribed.

In March, 1829, the Morris Canal and Banking Company, having obtained authority from the State of New Jersey to borrow $500,000 on their post-notes and to pledge the canal with its appurtenances and all the chartered rights of the company for the payment of the principal and interest of the loan, asked the bank to subscribe to the new loan, agreeing to take in payment for so much of the subscription the post-notes ($25,000) already held by the bank, and which would soon become due. The directors authorized a subscription for $25,000 on the above condition, and further that the whole amount of $500,000 should be subscribed for, and the security be made equal to that already held by the bank.

This indebtedness of the Morris Canal and Banking Company was paid at maturity, by draft on William Willink, Jr., Amsterdam, payable in London, for eight thousand pounds sterling, from which it seems likely that the canal company negotiated a loan in Amsterdam for the payment of their post-notes.

In April, 1829, a general banking law was passed which was known as the Safety Fund Act. By the provisions of this act the banks were authorized to issue circulating notes to twice the amount of their capital, and their loans were limited to twice and one half their capital. A common fund was established by a provision requiring every banking corporation thereafter organized, whose charter should be renewed or extended, to pay annually to the treasurer of the State a sum equal to one half of one per cent. of its capital stock paid in; such payments to be continued until each bank had paid into the treasury three per cent. of its capital. The fund thus created was made applicable to the payment of the circulation and other debts of any insolvent bank contributing to the same.

An act was passed in January, 1831, extending the charter of the Bank of New York to January 1, 1853, except such parts thereof as might be repugnant to the provisions of the general act above referred to, and providing that the provisions of said act should be accepted by the board of directors of the bank. This was complied with, and the bank went into operation under the provisions of the new act.

During the month of August, 1832, a letter was received by the directors of the bank from Amos Kendall, stating that he had been appointed by the Secretary of the Treasury, at the request of the President of the United States, to confer with the state banks in relation to the future deposit and distributing of the public revenue. It was deemed probable by the government, he said, that the Bank of the United States would not be re-chartered, and that no other institution would be established by Congress to supply its place as an agency of the treasury. And as the government would wish to employ another agent, or other agents, he wished to ascertain on what terms the Bank of New York would undertake the agency, or a portion of it.

The president of the bank had a personal interview with Mr. Kendall, and, after consulting with the directors, informed him that as the bank was under the operation of the Safety Fund Law of New York, the loans were limited to two and a half times the amount of its capital, and the deposits being large, the directors were enabled to extend the loans and discounts to nearly the amount allowed by law. The bank would, therefore, be unable to profit by any amount of deposits which the secretary might leave in its possession. The directors, therefore, declined the proposed service; but offered to hold any part of the public funds which the secretary might choose to deposit in the bank, subject to his order, payable in New York, Boston, Philadelphia, or Baltimore.

On the 5th of August, 1832, Charles Wilkes resigned the presidency of the bank on account of continued ill health; and the severance of his connection with the institution which he had served so faithfully for forty-eight years was the occasion of deep regret on the part of the directors.

Charles Wilkes was born in London, August 30, 1764. He came to this country in 1784, at the suggestion of William Seton, with whom his family were on terms of intimacy. Soon after the organization of the Bank of New York he entered its service, and in 1792, while acting as teller, he was appointed cashier of the Branch Bank of the United States, then just established in New York. He declined the appointment, and was shortly afterward elected assistant cashier of the Bank of New York. In 1794 he was elected cashier. The duties of this office were discharged by Mr. Wilkes with signal ability and devotion to the interests of the bank, and the directors repeatedly testified their appreciation of his services. In May, 1802, he asked for leave of absence, stating to the board that urgent family business rendered it indispensably necessary for him to go to Europe. A vacation of six months was accordingly given him, and the time was afterward extended to the following May. The occasion of this visit was a legacy which had been left him by a comparatively unknown relative in England, and which he voluntarily divided with his brother in this country. This act of generosity gave to the re-

Chas Wilkes

PRESIDENT 1825-1832

cipient of the gift what in those days was a handsome fortune.

The successful accomplishment of Mr. Wilkes's mission to London in behalf of the bank has already been referred to. He was president of the bank from 1825, and upon his resignation in 1832 the directors, in a letter to him, expressed their "high sense of his long continued services in behalf of the institution, distinguished as they have been for zealous fidelity, sound discretion, and unblemished integrity."

Mr. Wilkes died in 1833. His genial disposition and winning manners won for him the affectionate regard of all who knew him. He left six children, the eldest of whom married Francis Jeffrey, afterward Lord Jeffrey, who visited this country in 1813.

At the meeting of the directors on the 15th of November, Cornelius Heyer was elected president to fill the vacancy made by the resignation of Mr. Wilkes.

The increase of business in the city of New York, and the prospective withdrawal of a large amount of capital by the Bank of the United States, led the directors of the Bank of New York to petition the Legislature, in December, 1835, for liberty to increase its capital to $2,000,000, but the petition was not granted.

In 1836 the financial situation had become so serious that the Legislature of the State of New York passed a bill, in February of that year, for the relief of the city of New York, which authorized the banks, under the Safety Fund Act, to make foreign loans and use the money thus borrowed as capital. Taking advantage of this privilege, the Bank of New York effected a loan with Messrs. Morrison, Cryder & Co., of London, through Mr. Richard Alsop, their agent in New York, of £112,500 for thirteen months, at five per cent. interest; the bank giving its bonds for the amount, payable in London in two, three, and four years, with interest warrants attached. The bonds were to be sold by Messrs. Morrison, Cryder & Co., and the proceeds applied to the liquidation of the principal and the accruing interest of the loan. The negotiation of this loan was reported to the comptroller of the State and the bank commissioners.

The difficulties which had already proved so embarrassing were increased by the fact that the Bank of New York was called upon, in May, 1836, to return to the Bank for Savings $300,000, which it had held on special deposit for that bank for a considerable time. Fortunately, on the 4th of May, the commissioners of the canal fund offered to the bank $100,000 at five per cent., to be repaid on the 1st of July, 1837; and on the 23d of August the receivers of the Washington Insurance Company also made to the bank a loan of $194,000 at five per cent., to be repaid on twenty days' notice.

On the 24th of April, 1837, the commissioners of the canal fund asked for proposals for a loan of $3,-395,000, mostly at five per cent. interest; and a combination of banks in the city of New York agreed to take the whole amount in proportion to their capital. But the offer as made was not satisfactory to the comptroller of the State.

In October of the same year the commissioners decided to issue to the Bank of New York transferable certificates of stock to the amount of $200,000, bearing five per cent. interest, upon certain conditions, which were complied with by the bank, and the stock was afterward sent to London for sale.

The financial embarrassment had increased during the month of April, 1837, and the officers of the New York banks held repeated meetings for the purpose of consultation. On the 9th of May it was resolved to suspend specie payments, and a series of rules and regulations for mutual protection were adopted, to continue in force during the period of suspension.

On the 27th of November, 1837, a convention composed of 136 delegates representing banks in all parts of the country was held in New York to take measures for an early resumption of specie payments. Messrs. Albert Gallatin, George Newbold, Cornelius Heyer, president of the Bank of New York, and others were appointed a committee to publish the views of the convention. Another meeting of the convention was held on the 11th of April, 1838, and a resolution passed to recommend the banks to resume specie payments on the first Monday in January. This, however, was found to be impracticable.

The banks of New York finally resumed on the 10th of May, 1838. Those of Pennsylvania and the Southern States followed on the 13th of August, but were unable to maintain specie payments, and on the 9th of September, 1839, again suspended.

In December, 1840, an application was made to the Bank of New York by a committee of the Philadelphia banks for a loan to enable them to resume specie payments, but it was decided that it was inexpedient to make the loan at that time. The Philadelphia banks were then largely indebted to the banks in the city of New York, and the latter found it difficult to maintain specie payments. In 1841 the necessity of again suspending was freely discussed, but such a course was strongly opposed by the larger banks. These sold their claims on Philadelphia at as high a rate of discount as thirteen per cent. Mr. Newbold, of the Bank of America, brought on at one time from Philadelphia $400,000 in specie, which enabled the banks of this city to maintain specie payments.

The Bank of New York during this period of great stringency in the money market extended material aid to the State. On the 1st of April, 1840, it lent the commissioners of the canal fund $200,000 for ninety

Corn^l. Heyer

PRESIDENT 1832-1843

days, and in the following June, $200,000 more for six months. In May, 1843, the bank subscribed for $150,000 New York six per cent. stock, payable at the pleasure of the commissioners of the canal fund after the year 1860.

The office of president of the bank was made vacant by the death of Cornelius Heyer on the 5th of January, 1843. Mr. Heyer was for fifty-two years in the service of the bank. He was born in 1773, and entered the bank at the age of eighteen. After acting as teller he resigned the position and entered into mercantile business; but at the invitation of the officers of the bank he resumed his position in it. He was appointed cashier in 1825, and succeeded Mr. Wilkes as president of the bank in 1832. Mr. Heyer was highly esteemed as a valuable member of the church and of the community. He was for many years president of the Board of Corporation of the General Synod of the Reformed Dutch Church, and was prominent in her various councils.

At the next meeting of the directors of the bank, John Oothout was chosen president.

During this year the bank sustained another loss in the resignation of Joshua Waddington, who had been identified with the institution as a director since 1784. In a letter to the directors on the 6th of June, 1843, Mr. Waddington stated that, having reached a period of life which made it difficult to continue his punctual attendance at the bank, he felt constrained to resign the office he had held for nearly sixty years.

Mr. Waddington died on the 29th of February, 1844, in his ninetieth year. He was a native of England, and had been in business there before coming to this country. During his long residence in New York he was universally respected and esteemed.

It is an interesting fact that Mr. Waddington's term of service as director of the Bank of New York and that of Charles E. Bill, now senior director, cover every year of its existence. Mr. Waddington was elected a director at the first meeting of the subscribers in 1784, and continued to serve until 1843; Mr. Bill has held his office since 1837.

# CHAPTER VIII

## 1852–1884

*Expiration of the Charter of the Bank. — Reorganization under the Free Banking Act in 1853. — Increase of Capital to $2,000,000 in 1853. — The Panic of 1857. — Suspension of Specie Payments by the Banks in October, 1857. — An Injunction asked for against the Bank of New York. — Decision in Favor of the Bank. — Resumption of Specie Payments in December, 1857. — The New Bank Building completed in 1858. — Death of John Oothout in 1858 and Election of Anthony P. Halsey as President. — The War of the Rebellion. — Increase of Capital to $3,000,000 in 1859. — A Loan Committee appointed in 1860. — Financial Aid extended to the Government by the Bank of New York. — Death of Anthony P. Halsey in 1863 and Election of Charles P. Leverich as President. — Organization of the Gold Department of the Bank in 1864. — Reorganization of the Bank under the National System in 1865. — Retention of its Former Title. — Death of Charles P. Leverich and Election of Charles M. Fry as President in 1876. — Reduction of Capital to $2,000,000 in 1878. — Dividends paid by the Bank during its Existence. — Conclusion.*

IN May, 1852, when the charter of the bank was about to expire, books were opened for subscriptions to a new bank under the general banking law known as the Free Banking Act, and passed in 1838. The capital of the new bank was fixed at $2,000,000 in shares of $100 each; the stockholders of the old bank being entitled to subscribe to twice the amount of their stock, and only one half of the additional capital being required to be immediately paid in.

The stockholders of the bank having subscribed to

the articles of association in accordance with the requirements of the statute, and the requisite security having been deposited with the Banking Department at Albany, the Bank of New York, on the 1st of January, 1853, became a free bank, with the directors, officers, and clerks of the previous bank. The assets and liabilities of the old bank had been sold and conveyed to it by deed of transfer. The real estate on the corner of Wall and William streets was valued at $250,000. A careful estimate of the cash value of the assets in excess of the capital was made, and a final dividend of thirty-eight and one half per cent. was declared, which dividend was receivable in payment of subscriptions to the new bank. It was estimated that the circulation of the bank which was lost or destroyed, and which would never be presented for redemption, amounted to $50,000. The subsequent return of notes reduced the estimate to $40,000.

The financial stringency which existed in the fall of 1857 occasioned a good deal of apprehension. Several conferences were held by bank officers in New York to devise means of relief, and the Secretary of the Treasury was applied to for aid, but without success. The stringency continued, and finally culminated in a general suspension of specie payments on the 15th of October. The panic of that day might possibly have been prevented by an earlier agreement on the part of the banks to suspend specie payments, but each bank was desirous to be the last to propose such action. It was not until some of the banks out of Wall Street were reported to have suspended that the larger banks decided that they must protect themselves, and instead of the usual certification they certified checks as being "due the depositor." This action created distrust and made depositors more anxious to receive gold for their checks.

A crowd filled the banking-room of the Bank of New York, and as it became evident that gold was being drawn on checks which should properly have gone through the clearing-house, it was decided, at about 2 P. M., to refuse payment of any checks or bills not presented by a dealer in the bank.

On the 13th of October, during the run on the banks, a person presented two one-hundred-dollar notes of the bank to the paying teller and demanded the specie, which was refused.

Application was immediately made by the holder of the notes to the Supreme Court for an order to show cause why an injunction should not be granted against the bank and a receiver appointed.

The case was argued before Judge Roosevelt, who decided against the application, on the ground that while a bank may refuse to redeem its circulating notes during a period of general suspension, that refusal of itself does not prove that the bank is insolvent; the bank having at the time property not only sufficient but in every respect more than sufficient to satisfy all demands. Within the meaning of the statute, therefore, it is clearly solvent.

The suspension was of short duration. On the 13th of November the board of directors of the Bank of New York passed a resolution to the effect that the bank was ready for a general resumption of specie payments, and only awaited the action of the banks of the city and the State to carry the measure into effect. They further resolved to resume specie payments for all small notes of the bank then in circulation. On the 11th of December the president signed an agreement with the other banks of the city to resume specie payments for all their obligations on the following Monday. Specie payments were accordingly resumed on the 14th of December, 1857.

The need of better accommodation for the business of the bank had long been felt, and in 1856 a committee had been appointed to procure plans for a new building. The plans submitted by Messrs. Vaux and Withers were subsequently adopted, and the bank was temporarily removed to the second story of the building occupied by the Bank of the State of New York, at the corner of William Street and Exchange Place. The old building was torn down and a new one erected, four stories in height, having a front of thirty-eight feet, and a depth on William Street of one hundred and twenty-six feet. The cost of the structure was

BANK OF NEW YORK
B
The President Directors & Co.
of the Bank of NEW YORK Promise to pay
ONE Dollar on Demand
or bearer
Cash
Pres
ONE
Bank of New York
ONE DOLLAR
New York
Cash
Pres

$173,400. The corner-stone was laid on the 10th of September, 1856, and the structure completed early in 1858; and on the 29th of March business was begun in the new building.

The structure was described at the time as "built in the Italian style, of Little Falls brown stone and Philadelphia brick. The banking-room is fifty-eight feet long, thirty-five feet wide, and twenty-six feet high, occupying two stories in the central and rear part of the building. The ceiling and walls, and the whole fitting-up of the interior compare favorably with the elegance of the exterior, and the room is lighted on the east side, where it adjoins the present American Exchange Bank, by glazed panels in the ceiling. The front part of the building on Wall Street and the upper stories are intended for offices, and the whole is constructed with iron beams and concrete, so as to be completely fireproof." By a novel and ingenious arrangement an abundance of light was given to the upper story, and the bank was thus enabled to let that part of the building to the clearing-house for a number of years.

So well satisfied were the directors with the building, that, at a meeting of the board, it was resolved, "that the consummate skill exhibited by the architect, Mr. Calvert Vaux, in the erection of the new banking-house deserves more than the mere acknowledgment that the board have been most fortunate in the selection of a comparative stranger to do the work," and an addition of $1500 was made to the sum already paid for his services.

The old clock, which for more than sixty years had kept time in the bank, was presented to the New York Historical Society, and was received as a gift possessing peculiar historic interest.

In 1858, the bank was again deprived by death of the services of one of its presidents. John Oothout, who had filled the office for fifteen years, died on the 29th of January. Mr. Oothout was born in the city of New York in 1789. He received his business education in the office of Robert Lenox, one of the most prominent merchants of that time. After the death of his father he left Mr. Lenox, but never engaged in mercantile business. In 1823 he became treasurer of the Chambers Street (now Bleecker Street) Savings Bank, and served that institution faithfully until 1843, when he resigned. He was elected a director of the Bank of New York in 1819, and was made president of the institution in 1843.

Mr. Oothout was also interested in many of the charitable institutions of the city. He was a man of the strictest integrity, and had the respect of all with whom he had business relations. Gentle in his manners and kindly in his feelings, he was universally beloved and his death deeply lamented.

The directors of the bank at their meeting on the

J. Oothout

PRESIDENT 1843-1858

2d of February elected Anthony P. Halsey president, in place of Mr. Oothout.

A demand for increased banking facilities in the city had existed for some time, and in 1857 the directors of the Bank of New York had decided to increase the capital of the institution to $3,000,000; the additional amount to be called for in installments. This was accordingly done, and by July, 1859, the whole amount was paid in.

In the fall of 1860 it became evident that a financial crisis was near at hand. A civil war was threatened, and in November the first of the loan committees, formed by the associated banks for the purpose of facilitating their action in behalf of the United States government, began its labors. Of this the vice-president of the Bank of New York was a member, and also custodian of the securities entrusted to it. This committee continued its labors until March, 1861, when its term of service expired by limitation. Another committee was then formed, which continued in existence until May 1, 1862. The committee met weekly in rooms on the third floor of the Bank of New York building, which were set apart for their use. The whole amount of loan certificates issued by the committees from April 29, 1861, to May 1, 1862, was $22,585,000. The largest amount outstanding at any one time was $21,960,000. These certificates were issued on the pledge of the United States Treasury notes and coupon and registered stock, which the banks were entitled to receive from the treasurer of the United States.

The magnitude of the responsibility entrusted to this committee is apparent from the fact that they received from the United States treasurer, during this time, cash to the amount of $105,434,903, all of which had to be counted and apportioned among the banks.

Toward the close of the year 1860, the outlook was so threatening that a meeting of bank officers was called on the 28th of December at the office of the assistant treasurer of the United States, in New York. The financial situation was fully discussed, and it was resolved to suspend specie payments on the following Monday. This action was not at first acceded to by a majority of the banks, as they were under contract with the government to take their proportionate amount ($35,000,000) of the $50,000,000 United States bonds on which several installments had already been paid, but it was finally agreed to by all the banks.

The Bank of New York took a prominent part in all the measures for the relief and support of the government throughout the war of the rebellion. It was represented in all the meetings of the officers of the associated banks in relation to financial aid to the government at the beginning of the war, by Charles P. Leverich, its vice-president, who was made the custodian of the securities deposited with the loan com-

mittee. The bank subscribed for its proportion of the hundred millions of United States 7.30 treasury notes which were taken by the banks of New York, Philadelphia, and Boston in 1861, and also for its proportion of the fifty millions of United States six per cent. bonds.

In April, 1861, the bank subscribed $50,000 to the city loan for equipping volunteers, and in March, 1862, $15,000 for the defence of the city. In September, 1863, the associated banks were again appealed to by the treasurer of the United States to subscribe for thirty-five millions of bonds. The loan was made, the Bank of New York taking its proportion of it. In June, 1864, the bank held upward of three millions of United States bonds and state and city stocks.

On the 11th of May, 1863, Anthony P. Halsey resigned the office of president of the bank on account of failing health. His resignation was accepted on the 14th, and Charles P. Leverich elected to fill the vacancy.

Mr. Halsey died on the 26th of August, at the age of sixty-nine. He had been connected with the bank for forty-seven years. His business education was begun in the counting-room of Messrs. Isaac Moses & Co., but he decided to turn his attention to banking, and entered the Bank of New York. During his long connection with this institution he filled the position of clerk, teller, cashier, vice-president, and president with eminent ability. He was prominent in the development of the public-school system of the city, and actively interested in Sabbath-schools, devoting much time to their advancement, and contributing liberally to their support. He was a ruling elder in the Pearl Street Presbyterian Church, and afterward in the Central Church; and a minute in the records of the General Assembly of that denomination recognizes his valuable services as treasurer of the Assembly, of the Church Erection Fund, and of the Union Theological Seminary, and pays a high tribute to his Christian character.

In 1864, the gold coin in circulation having become much depreciated by clipping, filing, and filling with a baser metal, the board of gold dealers, through their president, H. M. Benedict, requested the Bank of New York to organize a department for the examining, bagging, and sealing of gold coin, against which checks should be certified by the bank for $5000 each; such checks to be a legal delivery for so much gold. In compliance with this request, a gold department with thirty-seven subscribers was organized on the 16th of December, 1864.

Paul Bunker, then the oldest clerk in the bank, and who had filled the positions of paying teller and assistant cashier, was appointed manager of the gold department. W. D. Matthews and John Aschille were appointed expert examiners, and ten iron safes were constructed in the vault for the safe keeping of the gold coin.

This department increased rapidly; and on the 4th of April, 1865, fifty-two gold dealers and fifty-five merchants had become subscribers. The amount of gold coin deposited to be examined, sifted, and tested in various ways assumed such proportions that, in a little over three months, the amount examined and bagged was $41,243,000.

On the third floor of the bank large rooms had been furnished for the business, with scales of great sensitiveness and accuracy. Pieces of different denominations were separated by passing the coin through a series of sieves. Suspicious pieces were tested and weighed separately; and it is believed that no bad or light coin passed out in the bags put up and sealed at the bank.

Mr. Aschille having resigned his position, E. H. Birdsall was appointed chief examiner, and John A. Cisco, assistant. Both of these gentlemen came from the assistant treasurer's office in New York, and were unequalled as experts.

The permanent deposit of coin amounted to $11,000,000, which remained in the keeping of the bank until August, 1865. At about that time the United States Treasury began the issue of gold notes against deposits of coin. The deposits by the gold dealers in the bank were speedily drawn out, but the gold department was continued until the resumption of specie payments on January 1, 1879. On the last day of 1878 the gold accounts were written up and balanced; and by 11 o'clock P. M. all the balances had been transferred to the currency accounts of the dealers.

When the safes were constructed for the keeping of the gold, in 1864, twenty safes were also built in the upper vault for the use of customers of the bank. These were all rented early in 1865; and so great was the demand for this accommodation that one half of the lower vault was fitted up in the same way as quickly as possible, and during the next year it was found necessary to build vaults in the other half. In 1879 the bank built a safe-deposit vault in the basement, where there had been a check and box vault. The doors to this vault were constructed with great care; the outer one, which weighs three tons, is hung on a crane, but is opened and closed with perfect ease.

On the 6th of July the Bank of New York became a national bank, in accordance with the provisions of the National Banking Act passed by Congress in 1864, and took the title of "The Bank of New York National Banking Association," which it still retains. It was the earnest wish of the Secretary of the Treasury that the Bank of New York should become and be known as the First National Bank; but the directors were unwilling to part with the name under which the bank had been in successful operation for so many years. The plan of the Secretary was that each of the banks should take a numerical designation; but the proposition that the New York city banks should surrender their old names was not favorably received by them, and it was not until the Secretary consented that they might retain their former titles by adding the word "National" that the older banks changed from the state to the national system.

The panic of 1873 exceeded in severity any that had been known in New York. The failure of a prominent banking-house on the 13th of September in that year was followed by other failures of bankers, banks, and trust companies on the succeeding days, and by the closing of the Stock Exchange on the 20th. The condition of affairs was so serious that a meeting of bank officers was held on the 19th of September, at which Messrs. Charles P. Leverich, of the Bank of New York; F. D. Tappen, of the Gallatin Bank; H. F. Vail, of the Bank of Commerce; W. L. Jenkins, of the Bank of America; and M. P. Bryson, of the Phœnix Bank, were appointed an advisory committee to devise means of relief. A special committee was afterward appointed, of which Mr. Leverich was a member, who were authorized to issue clearing-house certificates to the amount of $10,000,000 on deposits with them of stocks. Seventy-five per cent. was advanced on the market value of these securities, and the certificates were available until the 1st of November.

The banks also agreed to act as agents for the purchase of $10,000,000 of bonds which the United States sub-treasurer had offered to buy. These measures afforded the desired relief to the money market, and the panic was of comparatively short duration.

The bank sustained a serious loss in the sudden death, on the 10th of January, 1876, of its president, Charles P. Leverich, who had been closely connected with it for thirty-six years. A special meeting of the directors was immediately called, at which resolutions were passed, expressing their appreciation of his character, and their sorrow at his death.

The ancestors of Mr. Leverich came to this country from England in 1633, and settled at Newtown, L. I. He was born in that village on the 17th of July, 1809. At the age of eighteen he began the business career which proved so successful, and entered the house of Peter Remsen & Co., of which his elder brother, Henry S. Leverich, was afterward a partner. In 1833 he commenced business on his own account, and formed a partnership with Peter R. Brinkerhoff, which terminated at the end of the year. He then continued the business alone, dealt largely in sugar and cotton, and acted as agent for a large number of estates at the South. In May, 1840, he became a director in the Bank of New York; in February, 1853, he was elected vice-president; and in 1863 he succeeded Anthony P. Halsey as president of the institution.

C P Leverich

PRESIDENT 1863-1876

Mr. Leverich's devotion to the interests of the bank was as marked as his patriotic efforts in behalf of the government of the United States during the critical period of the civil war. These efforts were as unremitting as they were valuable. He was a member of the Committee of Safety, which was formed before the war, and was prominent in its councils. In November, 1860, the first loan committee authorized by the banks of New York, and which has already been referred to, was formed in New York. It consisted of Moses Taylor, James Punnett, Reuben W. Howes, and Charles P. Leverich. This committee represented the banks in lending to the United States government $50,000,000 to enable it to carry on the war; and the timely aid thus afforded at a most critical period was invaluable. Mr. Leverich was an active and useful member of the committee; and as custodian of the funds in its possession, he had under his sole charge the sum of upward of one hundred millions of dollars in securities which were lodged with him, and for which certificates were issued.

Mr. Leverich took an active part in the Clearing-House Association of the banks of New York, and in 1863 was elected its chairman, but declined the office. The directors of the Bank of New York had great difficulty in inducing Mr. Leverich to accept any compensation for his arduous and responsible services as its vice-president. In June, 1862, the board passed a preamble and series of resolutions setting forth that, as their frequent attempts to relieve themselves of the obligations they were under to him had been resisted with rare disinterestedness and singular pertinacity, they were unable longer to accept such valuable services without due return. The directors therefore unanimously decided to fix his salary at $5000, and to transfer one hundred shares of the stock of the bank to him as some evidence of their appreciation of his devotion to the interests of the institution while serving as vice-president for so long a period of gratuitous labor; assuring him that they could no longer dispense with his acquiescence in their intentions.

During his business career Mr. Leverich was a director in several corporations, among which were the Panama Railroad Company, with which he was for a long time connected, the Long Island, the Knickerbocker, and other insurance companies. He was also a trustee of the old Chambers Street (now the Bleecker Street) Bank for Savings; and was connected with a number of other institutions. His excellent judgment and his strength of character made him a safe counsellor, while his characteristics as a citizen, his public spirit, and his unostentatious charity won for him the esteem of the entire community. He was a member of the Fifth Avenue Presbyterian Church, of which the Reverend John Hall, D. D., is pastor; and one of the noble acts of his life was the building and giving to his friends and neighbors at Corona (West Flushing), L. I., in 1871, a chapel, to be forever used as a free church.

The death of Mr. Leverich occurred during the period of great depression in financial affairs which followed the panic of 1873; and the choice of his successor at such a critical time was a matter of special importance. On the 18th of January, 1876, Charles M. Fry was elected president by the unanimous vote of the directors. Mr. Fry was chosen to fill the position on account of his ability and his long experience as a merchant and financier. He is a native of Virginia, and has been engaged in business in New York since 1848. He was elected a director of the bank in 1874, and during the same year was made vice-president. Under his administration as president the bank has so prospered that its condition was never better than at the present time, and the market value of its stock has advanced from par to a premium of seventy-five per cent.

In July, 1878, the Bank of New York became a depository of the United States Treasury for the sale of the four per cent. bonds. It disposed of a large amount of these securities, and was afterward a member of the syndicate which subscribed for all the unsold bonds.

The policy of reducing the capital of the bank had for some time been under consideration. It was evident that there was an excess of banking capital in New York, and a meeting of stockholders was held on the 23d of September, 1878, to take action in the matter; 22,429 shares of stock were represented, and it was unanimously resolved to reduce the capital from $3,000,000 to $2,000,000. One million dollars was therefore repaid to the stockholders on the 1st of October following, and certificates for the reduced amount of stock issued to them.

In 1879 it was decided to add two stories to the building occupied by the bank, according to plans submitted by Messrs. Vaux & Radford, and the work was completed early in 1880, at a cost of $56,800. The excellence of the location and the improvements made in the building caused the offices in the additional stories to be immediately taken. The building is heated by steam, and although it is fire-proof, each floor is furnished with a length of hose connected with a tank in the attic and with a steam pump in the sub-basement. As a part of the improvements in the building, a safe-deposit vault was constructed in the basement, with all the latest devices for the safety of its contents. The outer door of the vault weighs three tons, and is closed by means of a lever with arrangements for making the interior air-tight.

The Bank of New York has never passed a dividend except in 1837, when it was obliged to do so by law. The records of the bank for the seven years pre-

PRESIDENT 1876 - 1892

ceding its incorporation are not in existence; but advertisements of dividends amounting to forty-five per cent. were published in the papers of the day, and it is probable that another dividend of three per cent. was made, of which no notice is to be found. A statement of the total amount of dividends can, therefore, be given.

| | |
|---|---|
| For the first six months after the incorporation the dividend was . . . . . . . . . . . . . | 7 % |
| For the next six months . . . . . . . . . | 4 % |
| From November, 1792, to November, 1823, inclusive, dividends of 4½ per cent. were made every six months, and four extra dividends at the same rate in 1794, 1797, and 1800; making in all . . . . | 301½% |
| From that time fifteen semi-annual dividends of 4 per cent. were paid, amounting to . . . . . . . | 60% |
| From November, 1831, to May, 1847, the rate of the semi-annual dividends varied from 3½ to 5 per cent., the regular dividend being passed in November, 1837, in compliance with the state law, as the banks had suspended specie payments. In May, 1838, however, after resumption, a dividend of 8 per cent. was made for the year. The dividends for the entire period, therefore, amounted to . . . . | 128½% |
| From November, 1847, to July, 1853, semi-annual dividends were regularly made of 5 per cent., amounting to . . . . . . . . . . . . . | 60 % |
| An extra dividend was also made at the close of the year of . . . . . . . . . . . . . . . | 38½% |
| From that date to the present time there have been seven dividends of 3 per cent., seven of 3½ per cent., twenty-one of 4 per cent., twenty-six of 5 per | |

cent.* and an extra dividend in January, 1884, of 2½ per cent.; amounting in all to . . . . . . . . 262 %

Amount of dividends made since incorporation . . 861½%

Add amount of dividends paid previous to incorporation . . . . . . . . . . . . . . . 48 %

909½%

The Bank has, therefore, paid to its stockholders during the one hundred years of its existence nine hundred and nine and one half per cent.

From November, 1823, to May, 1832, the state tax of six per cent. upon the amount of dividends was deducted from them when they were paid. But since the passage of the Internal Revenue Act, in 1868, the dividends have been paid free of all taxes.

Since the organization of the Bank of New York many distinguished men have had business relations with it. Among these were Talleyrand and Aaron Burr, fac-similes of whose checks are given in this volume. The names of many of the original stockholders still appear in the stock ledger of the bank, their shares having passed to their heirs, who still hold them. As the following statement would indicate, the stock is largely held as a permanent investment: —

| | | | |
|---|---|---|---|
| 235 women . . . . . . . | own | 6549 | shares. |
| 264 men . . . . . . . . . | " | 9945 | " |
| 56 trustees . . . . . . . | " | 2970 | " |
| 12 charitable associations . . | " | 536 | " |
| 567 stockholders . . . . . . | " | 20,000 | " |

VICE PRESIDENT 1882-1899

## The Bank of New York

In reviewing the history of the Bank of New York since its organization, those who are now or who have been associated with it may take a just pride in the position it has maintained through the changes of a century. It has survived the trials that have proved too severe for many other corporations, while the city whose name it bears has risen from a position of secondary importance to the rank of the chief city of the United States. And it can justly be said that of all the institutions of its kind that have grown up with it, none has more faithfully discharged its duty to the public, to the government, and to its stockholders, than the Bank of New York.

# Appendix.

# Appendix

## I

## LETTER OF ALEXANDER HAMILTON AND OF WILLIAM SETON

NEW YORK, *March* 21, 1784.

DEAR SIR: —

Permit me to introduce to your acquaintance and attention Mr. Seton, cashier of the Bank of New York. He is just setting out for Philadelphia to procure materials and information in the forms of business. I recommend him to you because I am persuaded you will with pleasure facilitate his object. Personally, I dare say you will be pleased with him.

He will tell you of our embarrassments and prospects. I hope an incorporation of the two banks, which is evidently the interest of both, has put an end to differences in Philadelphia. Here, a wild and impracticable scheme of a land bank stands in our way; the projectors of it persevering in spite of the experience they have, that all the mercantile and moneyed influence is against it.

Your obedient servant,

A. HAMILTON.

To MR. FITZSIMMONS.

PHILADELPHIA, *March* 27, 1784.

DEAR SIR: —

You will observe, by my letter of this day to our president, that I have been requested to postpone my visit to the bank until they shall be well informed that the Bank of New York has, or actually will obtain, a charter. Although I am confident this is only an ostensible reason for not wishing to see me at the bank, it will be highly necessary I should be regularly informed of what is doing in this respect, that I may be able to speak fully and with firmness to the subject; therefore, exclusive of any letter the directors may write to me, I trust you will communicate to me whatever may appear to you essential for me to know.

The fact is (and which cannot be communicated to the many, and therefore not mentioned in my official letter), their motive for not wishing to see me at the bank just now, arises from their being at present in very great confusion — the opposition of the new bank began it, and being pressed so hard by this opposition, they were obliged to lay themselves so open that it evidently appeared, if carried further, it would strike too fatal a blow. Therefore, for the safety of the community at large, it became absolutely necessary to drop the idea of a new bank, and to join hand in hand to relieve the old bank from the shock it had received. Gold and silver had been extracted in such amounts that discounting was stopped, and for the fortnight past not any business has been done at the bank in this way. The distress it has occasioned to those dependent on circulation and engaged in large speculations is severe; and, as if their cup of misery must overflow, by the last arrival from Europe intelligence is received that no less a sum than £60,000 sterling of Mr. Morris's bills, drawn for the Dutch loan, are under protest. It is well known that the bank, by some means or other, must provide for this sum. The child must not desert its parent in distress, and such is their connection that whatever is fatal to the one must be so to the other. However, the man who has more than once, by his consummate abilities, saved the American Empire from ruin, will no doubt be found equal to overcome these temporary inconveniences, and to restore universal confidence and good order. I trust you will be guarded in your conversation with others on this subject, lest it might recoil on me, and not only place me in a disagreeable situation, but defeat the purposes of my coming here.

I have had several interviews with our friend Gouv. Morris; he is for making the Bank of New York a branch of the Bank of North America, but we differ widely in our ideas of the benefit that would result from such a connection.

If it will not be intruding too much upon your time and goodness, may I request that you will now and then inform me what is doing by our Legislature, and permit me to assure you, that it will ever give me singular pleasure to have it in my power to evince the respect and esteem with which

I am, dear sir,

Your obedient and very humble servant,

WM. SETON.

ALEXANDER HAMILTON, ESQ.

## II

## COLONEL JEREMIAH WADSWORTH

### SECOND PRESIDENT OF THE BANK OF NEW YORK

Colonel Jeremiah Wadsworth was born in Hartford, Conn., July 12, 1743. Like his predecessor in the presidency of the bank, General McDougall, he followed the seas in early life, and became master of a vessel trading principally to the West Indies. At the age of thirty he relinquished this profession and settled down in his native town as a merchant. Being of an active disposition, and possessing remarkable business talents, he soon became a rising man. Silas Deane, writing from Paris to Mrs. Deane, in 1776, says: "Captain Wadsworth will carry my letters and papers, to whom I refer you for smaller matters. He is a valuable person, and I wish the public may become sensible of his worth."

On the breaking out of the Revolution, Wadsworth was appointed one of a commission to supply the Connecticut troops with stores and provisions. In December, 1776, he was made Commissary-General for the State. In the spring of 1778, Congress being then in session at Williamsburgh, he was sent for, and offered the position of Commissary-General of purchases. He accepted the office with great reluctance, and entered without delay upon its duties. He brought to his new position great energy, activity, and zeal, and the purest patriotism. The position, however, was too trying for his ardent temperament. He could not endure the conflicting orders and the long delays of Congress in supplying means for his department, and in failing health he resigned his office and retired from it in January, 1780.

On the arrival of Rochambeau during the following July, Colonel Wadsworth was appointed commissary for the French troops, which position he filled until the close of the war. After peace was declared, he went to France for the settlement of his claims against the French government. His accounts were so clear and accurate that they were settled without dispute or delay. While abroad he established business relations in Great Britain and France.

Returning to Hartford in the fall of 1784, he resumed his interest in commercial affairs, devoting much attention to agriculture, and studying the best means for its improvement. He became interested in manufactures, and with the coöperation of Oliver Wolcott, Oliver Ellsworth, and others, he established on his own premises the first woolen mill in the United States. The suit of clothes which Washington wore when he was first inaugurated was of cloth from this factory. Colonel Wadsworth had unrivaled talents for the transaction and dispatch of business. His observation was quick and accurate, and his memory strongly retentive. Of the men of his time he was one of the best acquainted with the resources of the country, and the best methods of utilizing them.

Colonel Wadsworth had also large legislative experience. He was several times elected to each branch of the Legislature of Connecticut, and was a delegate to the Continental Congress for three years. He was a member of the Connecticut Convention which ratified the Constitution, and strongly urged the adoption of that instrument. He was chosen to the first Federal Congress, and to the two next succeeding, holding his seat through Washington's first administration and half of his second. He was an intimate friend of Hamilton, and that great statesman received material aid from Wadsworth in shaping his plans for the financial and other material interests of the country. Colonel Wadsworth was early and largely interested in the establishment of banking in the United

States. While in the commissary department he had made the acquaintance of Robert Morris, which led to many business transactions between them. When the Bank of North America, in Philadelphia, was established in 1781, Wadsworth was the largest subscriber to its stock, taking 104 of the 1000 shares at $400 each. He also subscribed to the stock of the first Bank of the United States, of which he became a director. His connection with the Bank of New York was made at the solicitation of Hamilton. When the bank was organized in 1784, he was in Europe, where he had gone with John B. Church (to whom Hamilton addressed his letter of March 10, 1784), for the purpose of settling their accounts with the French government. Wadsworth and Church were partners in business. Hamilton and Church married sisters, — the daughters of General Schuyler.

The evidence as to the character and ability of Colonel Wadsworth is well supported by the testimony of two noted foreigners. The Chevalier de Chastellux, a general officer of the French army, who came over with Rochambeau, and who, with the latter, was frequently a guest of Wadsworth, describes him (in 1780) as "about thirty-two years of age, very tall and well made, and of a noble as well as an agreeable countenance. Throughout all America there is not a voice against him, and his name is never pronounced without the homage due to his talents and his probity." Brissot de Warville, the noted Girondist (guillotined in 1793) and friend of Lafayette, visited the United States in 1788, and on his return to France published an account of his travels. In writing of Hartford he says: "It is the residence of one of the most respected men in the United States, Colonel Wadsworth. He enjoys a considerable fortune, which he owes entirely to his own labor and industry. Thoroughly versed in agriculture and commerce, universally known for the services he rendered the American and French armies during the war, greatly esteemed and beloved for his great virtues, he crowns all his qualities by an amiable and singular modesty. His address is frank, his countenance open, and his desires simple. Thus you cannot fail to love him as soon as you see him."

Colonel Wadsworth was the originator and promoter of many public improvements in his native town; and the example he set was followed by his son, Daniel Wadsworth, who gave to the city of Hartford the noble and costly Athenæum which bears the family name and which is the most imposing and durable monument that could be reared to his memory. Colonel Wadsworth died April 30, 1804; his death preceding that of Hamilton about three months.

# III

## LIST OF THE PRESIDENTS AND CASHIERS OF THE BANK OF NEW YORK FROM ITS ORGANIZATION TO THE PRESENT TIME (1922)

### PRESIDENTS

| NAME | ELECTED | TERM OF OFFICE ENDED |
|---|---|---|
| Alexander McDougall, | June 9, 1784, | Resigned May 9, 1785. |
| Jeremiah Wadsworth, | May 9, 1785, | Resigned May 8, 1786. |
| Isaac Roosevelt, | May 8, 1786, | Resigned May 2, 1791. |
| Gulian Verplanck | May 11, 1791, | Died Nov. 20, 1799. |
| Nicholas Gouverneur, | Dec. 7, 1799, | Died July 14, 1802. |
| Herman Le Roy, | July 29, 1802, | Resigned May 8, 1804. |
| Matthew Clarkson, | May 8, 1804, | Resigned Apr. 13, 1825. |
| Charles Wilkes, | May 12, 1825, | Resigned Oct. 30, 1832. |
| Cornelius Heyer, | Nov. 15, 1832, | Died Jan. 5, 1843. |
| John Oothout, | Jan. 10, 1843, | Died Jan. 29, 1858. |
| Anthony P. Halsey, | Feb. 2, 1858, | Resigned May 11, 1863. |
| Charles P. Leverich, | May 14, 1863, | Died Jan. 10, 1876. |
| Charles M. Fry, | Jan. 18, 1876, | Died Nov. 18, 1892. |
| E. S. Mason, | Nov. 29, 1892, | Died Sept. 21, 1900. |
| Herbert L. Griggs, | Jan. 15, 1901. | |

### CASHIERS

| NAME | ELECTED | TERM OF OFFICE ENDED |
|---|---|---|
| William Seton, | Mar. 15, 1784, | Resigned June 10, 1794. |
| Charles Wilkes, | June 10, 1794, | Elected President May 12, 1825. |
| Cornelius Heyer, | May 12, 1825, | Elected President Nov. 15, 1832. |
| Anthony P. Halsey, | Nov. 15, 1832, | Elected Vice-President May 16, 1856. |

## The Bank of New York

| | | |
|---|---|---|
| William B. Meeker, | May 16, 1856, | Resigned Dec. 16, 1873. |
| Richard B. Ferris, | Dec. 19, 1873, | Elected Vice-President Jan. 12, 1882. |
| Ebenezer S. Mason, | Jan. 12, 1882, | Elected President Nov. 29, 1892. |
| Charles Olney, | Dec. 6, 1892. | April 15, 1912. (Elected Vice-President Jan. 12, 1910.) |
| Joseph Andrews, | Apr. 15, 1912, | Elected Vice-President Apr. 15, 1919. |
| Clifford P. Hunt, | Apr. 15, 1919, | Resigned Dec. 2, 1919. |
| Frederick C. Metz, Jr., | Dec. 2, 1919. | |

## IV

## LIST OF DIRECTORS OF THE BANK OF NEW YORK FROM ITS ORGANIZATION TO THE PRESENT TIME (1922)

| | TERM OF OFFICE |
|---|---|
| SAMUEL FRANKLIN | 1784 to 1796 |
| WILLIAM MAXWELL | 1784 to 1791 |
| ROBERT BOWNE | 1784 to 1792 |
| NICHOLAS LOW | 1784 to 1792 |
| COMFORT SANDS | 1784 to 1798 |
| DANIEL MCCORMICK | 1784 to 1799 |
| ALEXANDER HAMILTON | 1784 to 1788 |
| ISAAC ROOSEVELT | 1784 to 1791 |
| JOSHUA WADDINGTON | 1784 to 1843 |
| JOHN VANDERBILT | 1784 to 1787 |
| THOMAS RANDALL | 1784 to 1792 |
| THOMAS STOUGHTON | 1784 to 1790 |
| JAMES BUCHANAN | 1786 |
| WILLIAM CONSTABLE | 1787 to 1792 |
| WILLIAM EDGAR | 1789 to 1793 |
| JOHN MURRAY | 1789 to 1794 |
| GULIAN VERPLANCK | 1791 to 1799 |
| RUFUS KING | 1791 to 1792 |
| WILLIAM BAYARD | 1792 to 1794 |
| NICHOLAS GOUVERNEUR | 1792 to 1802 |
| CHARLES SMITH | 1792 |
| GEORGE TURNBULL | 1792 to 1794 |
| GERARD BANKER | 1792 to 1793 |
| RICHARD VARICK | 1792 to 1794 |

| | |
|---|---|
| JOHN MCVICKAR | 1793 to 1796 |
| JOHN H. THOMPSON | 1793 to 1794 |
| CORNELIUS RAY | 1793 to 1794 |
| WILLIAM DEMMING | 1794 to 1819 |
| JOHN JONES | 1794 to 1795 |
| JOHN B. COLES | 1794 to 1826 |
| GEORGE DOUGLAS, JR. | 1784 to 1795 |
| WILLIAM SETON | 1795 to 1798 |
| HERMAN LE ROY | 1795 to 1820 |
| MOSES ROGERS | 1795 to 1796 |
| PETER SCHERMERHORN, SR. | 1796 to 1797 |
| DAVID M. CLARKSON | 1797 to 1798 |
| ARCHIBALD GRACIE | 1798 |
| WILLIAM M. SETON | 1798 |
| SAMUEL CORP | 1799 to 1805 |
| THOMAS MARLE | 1800 |
| CHARLES L. CAMMANN | 1800 to 1805 |
| PETER KEMBLE | 1802 to 1805 |
| MATTHEW CLARKSON | 1803 to 1825 |
| EDWARD LYDE | 1803 |
| JOHN ATKINSON | 1806 to 1810 |
| WYNANT VAN ZANDT, JR. | 1806 |
| NEHEMIAH ROGERS | 1807 to 1827 |
| JAMES LENOX | 1807 |
| NATHAN SANDFORD (State appointment) | 1808 |
| HENRY POST (State appointment) | 1808 |
| ISAAC LAWRENCE | 1810 |
| G. S. MUMFORD (State appointment) | 1810 |
| SAMUEL A. LAWRENCE (State appointment) | 1812 |
| PETER P. GOELET | 1812 to 1826 |
| PETER SCHERMERHORN, JR. | 1814 to 1852 |
| JOHN MASON | 1814 to 1831 |
| ISAAC HEYER | 1815 |
| CHARLES MCEVERS | 1816 to 1840 |

| | |
|---|---|
| John Oothout | 1819 to 1858 |
| Thomas Eddy (State appointment) | 1820 |
| Jacob Le Roy | 1820 to 1823 |
| Samuel Boyd (State appointment) | 1821 |
| Julian Ludlow | 1823 to 1826 |
| Robert Bayard | 1823 to 1827 |
| Gardiner G. Howland | 1825 to 1852 |
| Charles Wilkes | 1825 to 1832 |
| Robert Maitland | 1826 to 1837 |
| Henry Beeckman | 1826 to 1857 |
| William G. Thompson | 1827 to 1833 |
| Gurdon Buck | 1827 to 1839 |
| Arthur Tappan | 1827 to 1831 |
| Edward R. Jones | 1827 to 1839 |
| John H. Hicks | 1831 to 1837 |
| George S. Robbins | 1831 to 1837 |
| Cornelius Heyer | 1832 to 1843 |
| Robert Benson | 1833 to 1858 |
| Charles E. Bill | 1837 to 1888 |
| E. A. B. Graves | 1837 to 1866 |
| Joseph Sampson | 1839 to 1842 |
| Charles P. Leverich | 1840 to 1879 |
| Josiah Lane | 1840 to 1872 |
| James Marsh | 1842 to 1853 |
| Frederick Schuchardt | 1843 to 1875 |
| Lindley M. Hoffman | 1844 to 1861 |
| John A. C. Gray | 1852 to 1868 |
| Edward P. Heyer | 1853 to 1857 |
| Peter V. King | 1853 to 1881 |
| Ezra Wheeler | 1857 to 1871 |
| P. H. Holt | 1857 to 1874 |
| Anthony P. Halsey | 1858 to 1863 |
| Wm. Oothout | 1858 to 1871 |
| Gardiner G. Howland | 1858 to 1876 |

| | |
|---|---|
| John N. Bradley | 1858 to 1889 |
| James H. Banker | 1861 to 1873 |
| William Astor | 1864 to 1883 |
| James M. Constable | 1866 to 1900 |
| Benjamin G. Arnold | 1871 to 1880 |
| Henry Oothout | 1872 to 1877 |
| Charles G. Francklyn | 1872 to 1876 |
| Robert S. Holt | 1874 to 1877 |
| Charles M. Fry | 1874 to 1892 |
| Franklin Edson | 1876 to 1895 |
| Robert Bliss | 1876 to 1881 |
| Charles D. Leverich | 1876 to the present time |
| George H. Byrd | 1877 to 1902 |
| James Moir | 1878 to 1899 |
| Gustav Amsinck | 1879 to 1909 |
| Anson W. Hard | 1881 to 1914 |
| Henry B. Laidlaw | 1881 to 1902 |
| Darius O. Mills | 1881 to 1910 |
| Eugene Kelly | 1884 to 1894 |
| Charles E. Bill, 2nd | 1888 to 1889 |
| John L. Riker | 1889 to 1909 |
| W. H. Bradford | 1890 to 1890 |
| J. Kennedy Tod | 1890 to 1906 |
| E. S. Mason | 1892 to 1900 |
| John Crosby Brown | 1895 to 1909 |
| Henry C. Swords | 1895 to the present time |
| John G. McCullough | 1900 to 1915 |
| Wm. A. Read | 1900 to 1916 |
| Daniel A. Davis | 1901 to 1915 |
| Herbert L. Griggs | 1901 to the present time |
| George L. Rives | 1901 to 1917 |
| Wm. J. Matheson | 1902 to the present time |
| Gordon MacDonald | 1902 to 1908 |
| Anton A. Raven | 1906 to 1918 |

## A History of

| | |
|---|---|
| HENRY D. COOPER | 1908 to the present time |
| CHARLES OLNEY | 1910 to 1919 |
| OGDEN MILLS | 1910 to 1916 |
| JAMES BROWN | 1910 to 1916 |
| SAMUEL T. HUBBARD | 1910 to the present time |
| WILLIAM S. COFFIN | 1916 to 1917 |
| PHILIP T. DODGE | 1916 to the present time |
| EUSTIS L. HOPKINS | 1916 to the present time |
| ROBERT C. HILL. | 1916 to the present time |
| JAMES B. MABON | 1916 to the present time |
| OGDEN L. MILLS | 1916 to 1918 |
| WILLIAM H. TRUESDALE | 1917 to the present time |
| SAMUEL RIKER, JR. | 1917 to the present time |
| WALTER W. PARSONS | 1918 to the present time |
| FRANK C. MUNSON | 1919 to the present time |
| LOUIS F. KIESEWETTER | 1919 to the present time |

## The Bank of New York

### PRESENT BOARD OF DIRECTORS

### 1922

| | |
|---|---|
| Charles D. Leverich | 1876 |
| Henry C. Swords | 1895 |
| Herbert L. Griggs (President) | 1901 |
| William J. Matheson | 1902 |
| Henry D. Cooper | 1908 |
| Samuel T. Hubbard | 1910 |
| Philip T. Dodge | 1916 |
| Eustis L. Hopkins | 1916 |
| Robert C. Hill | 1916 |
| James B. Mabon | 1916 |
| William H. Truesdale | 1917 |
| Samuel Riker, Jr. | 1917 |
| Walter W. Parsons | 1918 |
| Frank C. Munson | 1919 |
| L. F. Kiesewetter (Vice-President) | 1919 |

# V

## ACT OF INCORPORATION

### STATE OF NEW YORK

*An Act to incorporate the Stockholders of the Bank of New York, passed March 21, 1791.*

WHEREAS, Isaac Roosevelt and others, associated as a Company, under the style of the President, Directors, and Company of the Bank of New York, by their petition presented to the Legislature, have prayed for the privilege of being incorporated, the better to enable them to carry on the purposes of their institution: Therefore,

*I. Be it enacted by the People of the State of New York, represented in Senate and Assembly, and it is hereby enacted by the authority of the same,* That all such persons as now are, or hereafter shall be, stockholders of the said bank, shall be, and hereby are, ordained, constituted, and declared to be, from time to time, and until the second Tuesday of May, which will be in the year one thousand eight hundred and eleven, a body corporate and politic, in fact and in name, by the name of the President, Directors, and Company of the Bank of New York; and that by that name they and their successors, until the said second Tuesday of May, one thousand eight hundred and eleven, shall and may have continual succession; and shall be persons in law capable of suing and being sued, pleading and being impleaded, answering and being answered unto, defending and being defended in all courts and places whatsoever, in all manner of actions, suits, complaints, matters, and causes whatsoever: And that they and their successors may have a common seal, and may change and alter the same at their pleasure; and also that they and their successors, by the same name of the President, Directors, and Company of the Bank of New York, shall be in law capable of purchasing, holding, and conveying any estate, real or personal, for the use of the said corporation.

*II. And be it further enacted by the authority aforesaid,* That a share in the stock of the said bank shall be five hundred Spanish milled dollars, or the equivalent therefor in specie; and the number of shares shall not exceed one thousand eight hundred, exclusive of any shares that may be subscribed on the part of this State, and subscriptions shall be kept open under the direction of the president and directors of the said bank until the said number of shares shall be filled, and the whole amount of the stock, estate, and property which the said corporation shall be authorized to hold, including the capital stock, or shares above mentioned, shall never exceed in value one million dollars.

*III. And be it further enacted by the authority aforesaid,* That the stock, property, affairs, and concerns of the said corporation shall be managed and conducted by thirteen directors, one of whom to be the president, who shall hold their offices for one year, which directors shall be stockholders, and shall be citizens of this State, and be elected on the second Tuesday of May in every year, at such time of the day, and at such place in the city of New York, as a majority of the directors for the time being shall appoint; and public notice shall be given by the said directors, in two of the newspapers printed in the said city, of such time and place, not more than twenty nor less than ten days previous to the time of holding the said election; and the said election shall be held and made by such of the said stockholders of the said bank as shall attend for that purpose, in their own proper persons or by proxy; and all elections for directors shall be by ballot, and the thirteen persons who shall have the greatest number of votes at any election shall be the directors, except as is hereinafter directed. And if it should happen at any election that two or more persons have an equal number of votes, in such manner that a greater number of persons than thirteen shall, by plurality of votes, appear to be chosen as directors, then the said stockholders hereinbefore authorized to hold such election shall proceed to ballot a second time, and by plurality of votes determine which of the said persons so having an equal number of votes shall be the director or directors, so as to complete the whole number of thirteen; and the said directors, as soon as may be after the said election, shall proceed in like manner to elect by ballot one of their number to be their president, and four of the directors which shall be chosen at any year, excepting the president, shall be ineligible to the office of director for one year, after the expiration of the time for which they shall be chosen directors. And in case a greater number than eight of the directors, exclusive of the president, who served for the last year, shall appear to be elected, then the election of such person or persons above the said number, and who shall have the fewest votes, shall be considered as void, and such other of the stockholders as shall be eligible, and shall have the next greatest number of votes, shall be considered as elected in the room of such last described person or persons, and who are hereby declared ineligible as aforesaid. And the president, for the time being, shall always be eligible to the office of director, but stockholders not residing within this State shall be ineligible, and if any director shall remove out of this State his office shall be considered as vacant. And if any vacancy or vacancies should at any time happen among the directors by death, resignation, or removal from this State, such vacancy or vacancies shall be filled for the remainder of the year in which they may happen by a special election for that purpose, to be held in the same manner as is hereinbefore directed respecting annual elections, at such time and place in the city of New York as the remainder of the directors for the time being, or the major part of them, shall appoint. And the first directors shall be Isaac Roosevelt, William Maxwell, Thomas Randall, Daniel McCormick, Nicholas Low, William Constable, Joshua Waddington, Samuel Franklin, Comfort Sands, Robert Bowne, Gulian Verplanck, John Murray, and William Edgar, and shall hold their offices respectively until the second Tuesday of May next.

*IV. And be it further enacted by the authority aforesaid,* That in case it should at any time happen that an election of directors should not be made on any day when, pursuant to this Act, it ought to have been made, the said corporation shall not, for that cause, be deemed to be dissolved, but that it shall and may be lawful, on any other day, to hold and make an election of directors, in such manner as shall have been regulated by the laws and ordinances of the said corporation.

*V. And be it further enacted by the authority aforesaid,* That each stockholder shall be entitled to a number of votes proportioned to the number of shares which he or she shall have held in his or her own name at least three months prior to the time of voting, according to the following ratios — that is to say, at the rate of one vote for each share not exceeding four, five votes for six shares, six votes for eight shares, seven votes for ten shares, and one vote for every five shares above ten; stockholders actually resident within the United States, and none other, may vote in elections by proxy.

*VI. And be it further enacted by the authority aforesaid,* That it shall be the duty of the directors to make half-yearly dividends of so much of the profits of the said bank as to them, or a majority of them, shall appear advisable; and that once in every three years, and oftener, if thereupon required, by a majority of the votes of the stockholders, to be given agreeably to the ratios hereinbefore established, they shall lay before the stockholders, at a general meeting, for their information, an exact and particular statement of the debts which shall have remained unpaid, after the expiration of the original credit, for a period of treble the term of that credit, and of the surplus of profits, if any, after deducting losses and dividends.

*VII. And be it further enacted by the authority aforesaid,* That the directors for the time being, or a major part of them, shall have power to make and prescribe such by-laws, rules, and regulations as to them shall appear needful and proper, touching the management and disposition of the stock, property, estate, and effects of the said corporation, and touching the duties and conduct of the officers, clerks, and servants employed therein, and touching the election of directors, and all such other matters as appertain to the business of a bank; and shall also have power to appoint so many officers, clerks, and servants, for carrying on the said business, and with such salaries and allowances as to them shall seem meet: *Provided,* That such by-laws, rules, and regulations be not repugnant to the constitution and laws of the United States, or of this State.

*VIII. And be it further enacted by the authority aforesaid,* That this State shall have a right to subscribe any number of shares to the said bank, not exceeding in the whole the number of one hundred, at any time when they shall by law authorize any person or persons for that purpose, and the State shall have a right to increase the number of shares and stock which the said corporation may hold, to the amount of the sum subscribed, if the number of shares hereinbefore limited shall be subscribed before such subscriptions shall take place on the part of the State.

*IX. And be it further enacted by the authority aforesaid,* That the total amount of the debts which the said corporation shall at any time owe, whether by bond, bill, note, or other contract, over and above the monies then actually deposited in the bank, shall not exceed three times the sum of the capital stock subscribed, and actually paid into the bank; and in case of such excess, the directors under whose administration it shall happen shall be liable for the same, in their natural and private capacities; but this shall not be construed to exempt the said corporation, or any estate, real or personal, which it may hold as a body corporate, from being also liable for, and chargeable with, the said excess; but such of the said directors, who may have been absent when the said excess was contracted, or who may have dissented from the resolution or act whereby the same was so contracted, may respectively exonerate themselves from being so liable, by giving immediate notice of the fact, and of their absence or dissent, to the mayor or recorder of the city of New York, and to the stockholders, at a general meeting, which they shall have power to call for that purpose: *And further*, It shall not be lawful for the said corporation to emit any notes, or contract debts, which shall be payable in the bills of credit emitted by the laws of this State.

*X. And be it further enacted by the authority aforesaid*, That the lands, tenements, and the hereditaments which it shall be lawful for the said corporation to hold, shall be only such as shall be requisite for its immediate accommodation, in relation to the convenient transacting of its business, or such as shall have been *bona fide* mortgaged to it by way of security, or conveyed to it in satisfaction of debts previously contracted in the course of its dealings, or purchased at sales upon judgments which shall have been obtained for such debts: *And further*, The said corporation shall not, directly or indirectly, deal or trade in buying or selling any goods, wares, merchandise, or commodities whatsoever, or in buying or selling any stock, created under any Act of the Congress of the United

States, or of any particular State, unless in selling the same, when truly pledged to it by way of security, for debts due to the said corporation.

*XI. And be it further enacted by the authority aforesaid,* That no transfer of the stock of the said corporation shall be valid or effectual in law, until such transfer shall be entered or registered in a book or books, to be kept for that purpose by the directors.

*XII. And be it further enacted by the authority aforesaid,* That the bills obligatory, and of credit, under the seal of the said corporation, which shall be made to any person or persons, shall be assignable by endorsement thereupon, under the hand or hands of such person or persons, and of his, her, or their assignee or assignees, and so as absolutely to transfer and vest the property thereof in each and every assignee or assignees successively, and to enable such assignee or assignees to bring and maintain an action thereupon, in his, her, or their own name or names; and bills or notes which may be issued by order of the said corporation, signed by the president, and countersigned by the principal cashier or treasurer, promising the payment of money to any person or persons, or his, her, or their order, or to bearer, though not under the seal of the said corporation, shall be binding and obligatory upon the same, in like manner, and with the like force and effect, as upon any private person or persons, if issued by him, her, or them, in his, her, or their private or natural capacity or capacities, and shall be assignable and negotiable in like manner as if they were so issued by such private person or persons.

*XIII. And be it further enacted by the authority aforesaid,* That this present Act of Incorporation shall in no wise be forfeited by any non-user whatever, at any time before the second Tuesday in May next, and that it shall, on that day, be lawful for the stockholders above mentioned to assemble for the purpose of carrying into effect the same; any want of notice in the manner above prescribed, to the contrary, in any wise notwithstanding.

*XIV. And be it further enacted by the authority aforesaid,* That this Act be, and is hereby declared to be, a public Act, and that the same be, for the time hereinbefore limited, construed in all courts and places, benignly and favorably, for every beneficial purpose therein intended.

# VI

## LETTER FROM ALEXANDER HAMILTON TO THE DIRECTORS OF THE BANK OF NEW YORK

TREASURY DEPT., *January 25, 1795.*

GENTLEMEN: —

You were so obliging as to cause it to be intimated that the payment of the loan of two hundred thousand dollars had of your Institution might be deferred if the service of the United States should require it.

It will be a great convenience to this Department to avail itself of the permission, so as to defer the reimbursement of the principal of that sum to a year from its commencement. The interest can be paid at such periods as are agreeable to you.

I cannot let slip this opportunity of thanking, for the last time, the directors of the Bank of New York for that decided, prompt support of my administration which they have upon every occasion given. It has made a lasting impression on my heart. With great consideration and esteem,

I have the honor to be,

Gentlemen, your obedt. servant,

ALEXANDER HAMILTON.

TO THE DIRECTORS OF
THE BANK OF NEW YORK.

# VII

## LIST OF STOCKHOLDERS OF THE BANK OF NEW YORK AT THE TIME OF ITS INCORPORATION IN 1791

The par value of the shares was five hundred dollars each, one half of which amount only had been called in.

| | |
|---|---|
| Joshua Waddington | 8 |
| Alexander Hamilton | 1½ |
| Aaron Burr | 3 |
| William Constable | 14 |
| Oliver Cromwell | 1 |
| Black Friars' Society | ½ |
| Herman Le Roy | 1 |
| Thomas Ludlow | 2½ |
| Nicholas Gouverneur | 5 |
| St. Andrew's Society | 6½ |
| Wm. Seton & Co. | 1 |
| Robert Lenox | 1 |
| Helena Scott | 1½ |
| Worshipful Master and Wardens of St. Andrew's Lodge | ½ |
| Peter Keteltas | ½ |
| Dominick Lynch | 5 |
| William Maxwell | 15 |
| John Delafield | 2 |
| John B. Coles | 2 |
| Nicholas Low | 8 |
| Daniel McCormick | 15 |
| David Masterton | 15 |
| Comfort Sands | 4 |
| John Vanderbilt | 4 |
| Isaac Roosevelt | 5 |
| Robert Bowne | 4 |
| Elting & Varick | 1 |
| Major John Laurence | 3 |
| Thos. Bridgers Bridgers | 4 |
| Elias Nexsen | 1 |
| Abraham Bradley and Ebenezer Huggin | 10 |
| Abraham Bradley | 2 |
| Daniel C. Verplanck | 12 |
| Henry King | 1 |
| David Gelston | 4 |
| Gulian Verplanck | 8 |
| Isaac Clason | 4 |
| Chamber of Commerce | 1 |
| Richard Harrison | 1 |
| William Henderson | 1 |

| | |
|---|---|
| James Watson | 4 |
| George Douglas, Jr. | 4 |
| Sheffield Howard | ½ |
| Pieter Johan Van Berckel | 9 |
| Abraham Baldwin | 9 |
| George Thatcher | 3½ |
| George Partridge | 2 |
| James Richmond | 1 |
| Samuel Ward & Bros. | 2 |
| Francis Lewis | 6 |
| Mary Daubney | 3 |
| John Bush | 3 |
| Robert and George Service | 7 |
| Blaze Moore | 12 |
| Willet Seaman | 1 |
| Anthony S. Bleecker | 2 |
| John Glover | 1 |
| Peter Schermerhorn | 1 |
| Daniel Phœnix | 4 |
| James & Alexander | 1 |
| Christopher and Lewis Lente | 2 |
| James Scott & co. | 1 |
| Alex. Robertson | 34 |
| Peter McDougall | 2 |
| James Farquhar | 1 |
| George Fisher | ½ |
| Henry Newton | 2 |
| Hubert Van Wagener | 1 |
| John Shaw | 2 |
| Alexander Smith | 1 |
| Daniel Huger | 2 |
| Adonijah Huger | 1 |
| John Townsend & Co. | 2 |
| John Service, Jr. | 2 |
| John H. Thompson | 1 |
| John Franklin | 5 |
| John Bingham | 3 |
| Israel Wilkes | 1 |
| Alex. Macomb | 1 |
| William Minturn | 10 |
| Bartholomew Fisher | 1 |
| John Trafford | 4 |
| George Foose | 1 |
| Jane Byrne | 1½ |
| George Rapelye | 8 |
| William Husbands | ½ |
| Watson & Greenleaf | 2 |
| Daniel Penfield | 2 |
| Hugh McEwen | 3 |
| Augustin Lawrence | 2 |
| William Laight | 1 |
| Leonard Bleecker | 4 |
| Jacob Charles Souchay | 1 |
| Samuel Franklin | 5 |
| Joshua Sands | 2 |
| Peter Mesier | 1 |
| Jonathan Lawrence | 1 |
| Hayman Levy | ½ |
| Richard Varick | 7 |
| Richard Platt | 10 |
| James Leslie | 2 |
| Brothers, Coster & Co. | 1 |
| Nicholas Hoffman & Son | 1 |
| Gouverneur Kemble | 1½ |

Daniel Toocker . . ½
Murray & Sansom . . 6
John I. Roosevelt . . ½
Alexander Ross . . 10
Joseph Shippey & Co. . 1
Robert Gilchrist . . 3
Thomas McFarran . . 2
Reynier & John Suydam . . . . . . . . 1
Wm. Remsen & Co. . . ½
Maxwell & Berry, Attorneys for Ann Robertson . . . . 5
Lynch & Stoughton . 6
Hugh Gaine . . . . 3
Jacob Morrell . . . 1
Julia Bunyan . . . 2½
Ryerss & Reilly . . 1½
Robert Gosman . . . 2
John Fell. . . . . . 3
Daniel Ludlow . . . 2
William Willson . . 2
William Edgar . . . 4½
Thomas Morrell . . 3
Jonathan Morrell . . 3
Peter Allair. . . . 8
Robert Hodge . . . 12
Thomas Roach . . . 3
John Taylor . . . . 1
Mons. De La Forest . 5
George Turnbull . . 10
Sarah Robinson . . 3
Abraham Franklin . . 3
Peter Keteltas . . ½
Christopher Roberts . 5
Thomas Randall . . 5
Ann Mullen . . . . 3
James R. Smith . . . 2
Robert Stewart . . 5
Elie Jos. Chevalier . 2
Charles Smith & Co. . 4
Isaac Moses . . . . 1
Ann Van Horne . . 1
Cornelia Van Horne . 1
Mary Phillips . . . 1
Michael Price . . . 16
Theodosius Fowler & Co. . . . . . . . 3
Alexander Reinagle . 1
Richard Yates . . . 1
John Alsop . . . . 4
Thomas White . . . 1
John McVicker . . . 10
Wm. T. Robinson . . 3
Robert Chas. Johnson . . . . . . . 6
Walter Frazer . . . 3
David Lydig . . . . 2
Carlile Pollock . . 5
Trustees of the Mutual Assurance Co. of New York . . . 12
John McQueen . . . 3
Edmund Priar . . . 1
Garrit Harsin . . . 2
Robert North . . . 2
Elias Smith . . . . 2
Rufus King . . . . 12

# The Bank of New York

| | |
|---|---|
| John Murray | 1 |
| William Bayard | 1 |
| Ephraim Stoan | 8 |
| Robert Roberts | 2 |
| Lewis A. Scott | 2 |
| William Hill | 3 |
| Henry Sadler | 6 |
| Peter Kemble | 2 |
| Unus McIvers | 1 |
| Temperance Green | 25 |
| John Stevenson | 4 |
| John Baker | 4 |
| James W. Depeyster | 2 |
| James Anderson | 1 |
| Abijah Hammond | 9½ |
| John Ireland | 2 |

| | |
|---|---|
| Benjamin Martinius and Andreas Crommelin | 2 |
| Gulian Crommelin | 3 |
| Robert Daniel Crommelin | 2 |
| Richard Smith, Jr. | 4 |
| Josiah Ogden Hoffmann | 1 |
| Benjamin Seixas | 5 |
| Edward Griswold | 2 |
| George Gosman | 2 |
| Gilbert Aspinwall | 8 |
| Wm. S. Aspinwall | ½ |
| Anthony A. Rutgers | 1 |
| | 723 |

The Riverside Press
CAMBRIDGE · MASSACHUSETTS
PRINTED IN THE U.S.A.

www.ingramcontent.com/pod-product-compliance
Lightning Source LLC
LaVergne TN
LVHW010603110826
845149LV00003B/760

*9781418187439*